Defeating The Spirit of Jezebel

John Arcovio

Cover artwork by John Arcovio.

All Scripture quotations are from the King James Version of the Holy Bible unless otherwise noted.

Defeating The Spirit of Jezebel by John S. Arcovio

Published by Spirit Led Ministries Publishing
©2007

All rights reserved. No portion of this publication may be reproduced, stored in an electronic system, or transmitted in any form or by any means electronic, mechanical, photocopying, recording, or otherwise without the prior written permission of the author.

Printed in the United States of America.
First printing April, 2007
Second Printing May 2009
Third Printing March 2012
Fourth Printing January 2017

ISBN 978-0-9647343-6-4

For more information on other materials by John Arcovio, or to reorder materials, please contact:

Spirit Led Ministries, Inc.
1-888-776-0797
www.spiritled.net

Acknowledgments
Scripture Text

Chapter 1 1
Understanding Elijah and Jehu and Exposing Ahab and Jezebel

Chapter 2 33
Cultivating the Spirit of Elijah and Jehu

Chapter 3 89
Defeating the Spirit of Jezebel

SCRIPTURE TEXT

"Beloved, believe not every spirit, but try the spirits whether they are of God: because many false prophets are gone out into the world."
1 John 4:1

1
Understanding Elijah, Jehu – Exposing Jezebel and Ahab

Revelation 2:18-29:

"And unto the angel of the church in Thyatira write; These things saith the Son of God, who hath his eyes like unto a flame of fire, and his feet *are* like fine brass; ¹⁹I know thy works, and charity, and service, and faith, and thy patience, and thy works; and the last *to be* more than the first. ²⁰Notwithstanding I have a few things against thee, because thou sufferest that woman Jezebel, which calleth herself a prophetess, to teach and to seduce my servants to commit fornication, and to eat things sacrificed unto idols. ²¹And I gave her space to repent of her fornication; and she repented not. ²²Behold, I will cast her into a bed, and them that commit adultery with her into great tribulation, except they repent of their deeds. ²³And I will kill her children with death; and all the churches shall know that I am he which searcheth the reins and hearts: and I will give unto every one of you according to your works. ²⁴But unto you I say, and unto the rest in Thyatira, as many as have not this doctrine, and which have not known the depths of Satan, as they speak; I will put upon you none other burden. ²⁵But that which ye have *already* hold fast till I come. ²⁶And he that overcometh, and keepeth my works unto the end, to him will I give power over the nations: ²⁷And he shall rule them with a rod of iron; as the vessels of a potter shall they be broken to shivers: even as I received of my Father. ²⁸And I will give him the morning star. ²⁹He that hath an ear, let him hear what the Spirit saith unto the churches."

There are three spirits that are prevalent in this age. These three are the *spirit of Elijah, the spirit of Jehu, and the spirit of Jezebel.* The spirits of Elijah and Jehu are sent by the Spirit and working of God to confront and defeat the spirit of Jezebel. The spirit of Jezebel can manifest itself in many forms, but the main manifestation is seen in the efforts of "lay control." We will discuss other manifestations in more detail later. The spirit of Elijah is manifested through the ministry of the prophet and the true shepherd. Jezebel is against the family unit and seeks to destroy the family. The spirit of Elijah works in direct opposition to the spirit of Jezebel and ministers to bring healing to the family unit. This principle was prophesied to be one of the settings just before the coming of the Lord as is recorded in Malachi 4:5,6:

"⁵Behold, I will send you Elijah the prophet before the coming of the great and dreadful day of the LORD: ⁶And he shall turn the heart of the fathers to the children, and the heart of the children to their fathers, lest I come and smite the earth with a curse."

The spirit of Jezebel is neither male nor female in gender. We must acknowledge that spirits are genderless. We may refer in this book to the spirit of Jezebel by gender; nevertheless, the spirit of Jezebel has no gender. This spirit can attack male or female. It just so happens the very first person in the Scriptures this spirit influenced was a woman. This book will expose and explain some of the characteristics of the spirit of Jezebel working in a person's life individually or even in a church corporately. We will also cover how to cultivate the spirits of Elijah and Jehu to confront and conquer the spirit of Jezebel.

The spirit of Jezebel is a stronghold spirit that has many spirits that work under its influence. Some of these spirits are lust, rebellion, homosexuality, and lesbianism. We will deal with some of these in later chapters. We must recognize that while we are in the midst of a tremendous apostolic move of God, we also are facing some of the greatest spiritual battles the church has ever faced. As an overcoming Apostolic church anointed with the Spirit and demonstration of God, we should never be afraid to have people attend our services who have been influenced by demonic spirits. We are here to minister deliverance and healing to an outright wicked generation! Greater is He that is in us than he that is in the world! The more evangelistic a church is, the more it will have to deal with demonic spiritual powers. Never will it be more evident that a church does not have the overcoming anointing of God working in its midst than when a demonic spirit's manifestation begins to work in its midst. A church cannot challenge the demonic spirit realm if it does not have the goods. This principle is illustrated in the book of Acts 19:13-16:

"[13]Then certain of the vagabond Jews, exorcists, took upon them to call over them which had evil spirits the name of the Lord Jesus, saying, We adjure you by Jesus whom Paul preacheth. [14]And there were seven sons of one Sceva, a Jew, and chief of the priests, which did so. [15]And the evil spirit answered and said, Jesus I know, and Paul I know; but who are ye? [16]And the man in whom the evil spirit was leaped on them, and overcame them, and prevailed against them, so that they fled out of that house naked and wounded."

It is vital that the blood-of-Jesus-bought and spirit-filled church be an anointed, overcoming church that can offer deliverance to those bound by demonic spirits. We must receive the person who is being influenced by these spirits, salvage them, and send the demonic spirits packing! This is our anointed purpose!

In James 5:16-18, James reveals one key to obtaining the spiritual authority to defeat the spirit of Jezebel:

"[16]Confess *your* faults one to another, and pray one for another, that ye may be healed. The effectual (or the operative) fervent (heated) prayer of a righteous man availeth much."

This kind of prayer is effectual (operative) because it is fervent (heated). When you take water and heat it to the boiling point, it transforms into a gas form called "steam." Steam forms condensation, which gathers in the atmosphere in the form of clouds. When the clouds are full of enough condensation from the rising steam, then it falls back to the Earth in the form of rain. This natural principle parallels the spiritual principle of what occurs with heated, operative prayer! Job 36:27,28 records:

"[27]For he maketh small the drops of water: *they pour down rain according to the vapour thereof:* [28]Which the clouds do drop and distil upon man abundantly." (Emphasis added)

In 1999 there was a true report recorded of an area in Ethiopia near the border of Somalia that had gone three years without substantial rain. Severe drought was prevalent in the region, and much of the crops and livestock had perished. Thousands were facing the reality of starvation. A group of believers began to pray intercessory prayers for rain due to the region's grave situation. It was recorded that a natural convection formed over the Lake Victoria region with such force that water was sucked up into the atmosphere, and live fish were sucked up into the clouds. When rain began to fall in the region affected by the drought, fish also fell from the heavens. The prayers of those believers brought both food and water relief to the region![i]

Zechariah 10:1 also records:

"Ask ye of the LORD rain in the time of the latter rain; *so* the LORD shall make bright clouds, and give them showers of rain, to every one grass in the field."

There is a rare phenomenon of nature that occurs called the forming of a "super cell" storm. The super cell is the most dangerous of all storm cells because of the extreme weather generated by the intense updrafts and downdrafts. A super cell is formed when a small-scale low pressure system forms and a larger high pressure system collides with this low pressure system. Super cells often form near or immediately northeast of such a low pressure system. A recent story and movie was written and produced titled "The Perfect Storm," which captures this phenomenon. Paralleling this natural principle is the spiritual principle of the enemies' pressures and spiritual warfare tactics, which we will title "low pressure," and the intense call of God from on high to heated intercessory, operative prayer, which we will title "high pressure." When these two pressures collide, the atmosphere for an Apostolic "perfect storm" of Holy Ghost outpouring is created! The greater the pressure, the greater the storm! It is our divinely imparted mandate to answer the enemy's low pressure that he places upon our lives with high pressure created by our heated intercessory prayers!

We need to pray for spiritual "super cells" to form on the horizon of this generation! Heated, operative prayer is the key. It doesn't matter what kind of spirit comes against the church. Prayer is the key to overcoming the attacks of the enemy and truly being an overcomer! Jesus instructs us in Mark 9:29:

"And he said unto them, This kind can come forth by nothing, but by prayer and fasting."

When it seems you have come against a wall in a spiritual struggle, press forward with this understanding that the enemy's pressure is actually creating the climate needed for a spiritual outpouring! Sometimes the first prayer meeting does not accomplish all that is needed. Sometimes there must be "seasons" of focused prayer and fasting to see a stronghold broken! The enemy will attempt to discourage you in the midst of a lengthy trial to give up and "throw in the towel." We know that "this kind" can be broken through prayer and fasting!

Elijah was a man subject to like passions as we are. He prayed earnestly that it might not rain, and it rained not on the Earth for a space of three years and six months. Elijah's story begins in I Kings chapter 18. Elijah appears from the desert before the throne room of Ahab with a word from the Lord for Israel. It is vital that we understand where the spirit of Ahab fits in this end-time. The spirit of Ahab represents leadership that refuses to deal with the Jezebel spirit in a church body or an organization. Ahab represents leadership that "looks the other way" and empowers the spirit of Jezebel simply by doing nothing. This is what empowers the spirit of Jezebel and the leadership of Ahab.

The spirit of Jezebel does not seek for nor have any real authority. For Jezebel to operate, it needs an Ahab to work through. Jezebel mainly works through manipulation, lay control, deception, and seduction. Ahab himself did not kill any of the prophets, Jezebel did. The spirit of Ahab is too politically correct to ever be caught directly fighting the prophetic but, rather, will empower a person driven by the spirit of Jezebel to accomplish the "dirty work." The spirit of Ahab represents carnal, weak-willed, spineless, sugar-coated position and politically motivated leadership. The spirit of Ahab always turns a blind eye to unconfessed, hidden sin in leadership and has a lifetime membership card in the "good ole boys' club."

As I mentioned before, the spirit of Jezebel is genderless. Nevertheless, often the spirit of Jezebel will prey more on woman than men due to the natural fallen nature of women who find it easy to accomplish what they desire through emotional manipulation and seduction.

Many symptoms of a true man of God who is battling the spirit of Jezebel are: emotional and spiritual exhaustion (burnout), discouragement, "running in fear," and depression. In a true Apostolic Church, God raises the spirit of Jehu through intercessors who, with prayer and fasting, rise up and say, "Get your hands off our pastor and leadership." The spirit of Jehu is mainly seen through the spiritual operation of intercessors. The name Elijah has the meaning, "Yahweh is my God."[ii] The spirit of Elijah releases the spiritual and personal revelation of who God is.

The spirit of Elijah will operate within the ministry of the shepherd to reveal the spirit of Jezebel as well as through the operation and ministry of the prophet. This is one reason Jezebel hates the prophetic ministry – the possibility of exposure. There are three stages of attack by the spirit of Jezebel. First, flattery and seduction; second, manipulation both emotionally and spiritually; and, finally, persecution where the spirit attempts to discredit and destroy the true spirit of Elijah.

One operation that the spirit of Elijah fosters is true godly sorrow and repentance. Jezebel also despises repentance. The name Jezebel has the meaning "Baal exalts," "Baal is husband to," or "unchaste" (also from the words OT:336 iy (ee); not: and OT:2083 Zebul (zebool'); habitation, dwelling;) [iii]

The primary meaning of ba`al is "possessor."[iv] In a spiritual parallel, everything about Baal represents demonic oppression, obsession, and possession. Jezebel works directly under the influence of demonic power. A person under the influence of the spirit of Jezebel will not join himself/herself with anybody who does not join their attack, or anyone they cannot control, manipulate, or influence. The spirit of Jezebel depends on "cliques" to work through. A person who is being influenced by this spirit will only fellowship with those who are of "like spirit and mind." Often this person will even go to other saints, especially new believers, and give them a supposed "word of prophecy" or share something they are "deeply concerned about or praying about." That is divisive, manipulative, and sows discord followed by, "Now don't you tell Pastor; he doesn't need to know about this because he is very busy, etc." You better mark that person. Any true word or burden from God does not need to be hidden from spiritual covering! If anybody comes to you with a word for you and says, "Now we don't want to weigh Pastor down; he's very busy," you better step back and say, "Now wait a minute. I recognize this spirit, and this spirit does not bear the witness and testimony of Jesus."

In Revelation 19:10 when the angel of the Lord appeared before John the Revelator, he fell at his feet to worship him, but the angel forbid him:

"And I fell at his feet to worship him. And he said unto me, See *thou do it* not: I am thy fellowservant, and of thy brethren that have the testimony of Jesus: worship God: **for the testimony of Jesus is the spirit of prophecy.**" (Emphasis added)

The true nature and spirit of a prophetic word from God can be seen in its ability to stand under the closest scrutiny and revelation. Several of the following scriptural references support this truth.

Isaiah 48:16, "Come ye near unto me, hear ye this; *I have not spoken in secret from the beginning;* from the time that it was, there *am* I: and now the Lord GOD, and his Spirit, hath sent me." (Emphasis added)

Psalms 25:14, "The secret of the LORD *is* with them that fear him; and *he will shew* them his covenant." (Emphasis added)

Amos 3:7, "Surely the Lord GOD will do nothing, but *he revealeth his secret* unto his servants the prophets." (Emphasis added)

Luke 8:17, "For nothing is secret, *that shall not be made manifest;* neither *any thing* hid, that shall not be known and come abroad." (Emphasis added)

We need to be clear on where our loyalties are placed. This is especially true of those serving on the staff or leadership of a church. The spirit of Jezebel will test staff members to see where their loyalties lie and, if they sense that they are not totally loyal to their pastor, they will prey on this to gain a foothold. Revelation reveals how God feels about this. Revelation 2:22,23:

"22Behold, I will cast her into a bed, and them that commit adultery with her into great tribulation, except they repent of their deeds. 23And I will kill her children with death; and all the churches shall know that I am he which searcheth the reins and hearts: and I will give unto every one of you according to your works."

The adultery spoken of here is not necessarily sexual but, rather, emotional and spiritual. This is often observed in the area of our loyalties to the authority we serve with or to the assembly we attend. It can also be observed when a person chooses to counsel saints in the church and instruct them to "not bother Pastor about this issue," or to even pressure the person to keep the information "confidential" from the Pastor with the hidden motive of using the information to manipulate the person.

Spiritual adultery can be observed when a saint of God allows their spirit to "wander" from church to church with no true commitment to one particular assembly or shepherd. Spiritual adultery can be seen when a person will be in agreement and union with someone else to hide important facts concerning improper relationships and behaviors, keeping the truth from their pastor, leadership, or authority, which might be her husband. It's spiritual or emotional adultery to call a friend and share intimate and personal information about your life and not be open to your own husband or wife in sharing this information.

We must be cautious in joining ourselves to be one with someone else other than our spouse. Some cases of physical adultery begin first as seemingly innocent joining with someone of the opposite sex in prayer or personal counsel. It can even start from seemingly innocent friendships that cross the boundaries of intimate and romantic talk. That's how affairs start. We need to guard our heart from any relationship that allows us to be more open to the opposite sex than with our own spouse. You cannot become one in emotions with a person of the opposite sex and not go down the road of adultery eventually. We owe it to our spouses and families to be honest, true, and loyal. It does not matter how good a friend they are, don't go and talk about things that are humiliating to your spouse simply because you're upset with them. God's clear standard on spiritual and emotional adultery is recorded in Revelation 2:22,23:

"[22]Behold, I will cast her into a bed, and them that commit adultery with her into great tribulation, except they repent of their deeds. [23]And I will kill her children with death; and all the churches shall know that I am he which searcheth the reins and hearts: and I will give unto every one of you according to your works."

That's the bed you make when you lie with the spirit of Jezebel. Verse 23 – "And I'll kill her children with death, and all the churches shall know that I am He which searches the reins and hearts, and I will give everyone of you according to your works."

The New International Version reads like this:

"[22]So I will cast her on a bed of suffering, and I will make those who commit adultery with her suffer intensely, unless they repent of her ways. [23]I will strike her children dead. Then all the churches will know that I am he who searches hearts and minds, and I will repay each of you according to your deeds."

Another manifestation of the spirit of Jezebel is seen in an inordinate desire to control and manipulate people; often this is actually a form of witchcraft. I've seen family situations where the spirit of Jezebel influenced homes to the extent that a father or mother held unnatural control over their children for years, even beyond the age of teen or adulthood years. It is often the influence of the spirit of Jezebel that handicaps singles as they cross over into adulthood, yet still remain under the complete control of the parents, unable to make decisions on their own as adults. This oftentimes is carried over into marriage and creates marital strife.

I recall a true account of a newlywed couple that was living in a travel trailer at the end of the property where the husband's parents lived. Everyday this husband would be walking home from work and would pass his mother's house before arriving at the travel trailer where his precious bride was waiting his arrival. This sweet wife was usually hard at work cooking a fine meal for her newlywed husband. Unfortunately, as the husband passed his mother's house, his mother would invite him to come inside for some of her famous fried chicken, and the husband would unwisely oblige and eat until he was full. Consequently, when he would arrive home, to his wife's dismay, he was too full to enjoy the home cooked meal his bride had fixed.

Fortunately, through prayer and communication, this subtle influence of a spirit of Jezebel was confronted saving this couple a very rocky and disastrous marital path. The husband's mother, who was a very godly woman, probably did not even recognize the spirit of Jezebel that was attempting to cause her to manipulate and control her grown and married son. This is why it is important in dealing with the spirit of Jezebel to first expose this spirit by recognizing the bitter fruit of actions and responses it produces.

Let's go back to the book of Revelation 2:21-23. Even though the Ahab leadership of that day was willing to "wink" at the actions of Jezebel, God was not. The Ahab leadership actually empowered Jezebel by simply remaining silent and "looking the other way" as she killed the prophets with the sword, destroyed all the temples, and erected the idols of Baal. God deliver us from Ahab leadership! We do not know whether

Ahab was intimidated, afraid, or just plain didn't care. Nevertheless, Jezebel would have had no power if Ahab had not been in authority as king. This is one reason why, when the Jezebel spirit attempts to enter an assembly, it does not necessarily try to enter into a high profile position of leadership, but, rather, it targets leadership in a deceptive "behind the scenes manner." Its desire is to "influence leadership." The spirit of Jezebel always disguises itself at first with naïve and innocent presentations. In the beginning, a person under the influence of Jezebel will appear willing to work hard and do just about anything requested in the kingdom of God. Statements like, "I'm here for you," "I'm behind you," "I'm with you," seem to be the order of each day.

(I will pause here to warn readers not to become suspicious of anyone with a pure motive and spirit of service. Time always reveals the true motive of a person's heart. This is one reason why, as a pastor, I am careful to not move anyone who transfers to our church into a leadership position too quickly. Time is the revealer of all things. This principle is revealed in Nehemiah 7:3:

"And I said unto them, *Let not the gates of Jerusalem be opened until the sun be hot;* and while they stand by, let them shut the doors, and bar *them*: and appoint watches of the inhabitants of Jerusalem, every one in his watch, and every one *to be* over against his house." (Emphasis added)

Time is a revealer of all things. Nehemiah warned the inhabitants of Jerusalem not to open the gates at dawn or dusk. This was due to the low light conditions that would make it very difficult to identify who or what was attempting to enter the city. It is incredible the difference a night of prayer or waiting a few days on the Lord can make when faced with a difficult or high-pressure situation. We never go wrong choosing to wait on the Lord!)

Returning to the spirit of Jezebel, we understand that it uses emotional/spiritual manipulation to secure its influence with a leader and gain power to attempt to control that leader. This can also be observed in people who try to gain influence with leadership through monetary gifts. Jezebel will first try to seduce you. If that is unsuccessful, Jezebel will try to manipulate you through emotional and spiritual means. Finally, if neither of these works, then it will launch an all-out attack, intimidation, and even an assassination attempt on your character.

I've observed spouses afraid to confront the spirit of Jezebel rising up in their home because their spouse attempts to intimidate, embarrass, and humiliate them. Many mistakenly assume that if they just ignore the spirit and keep silent to keep the peace they are doing the "Christian" thing. Actually, they are embracing Ahab leadership and making matters worse! You need to rise up as a leader in prayer and fasting and ask God for courage and wisdom to confront! I am not talking about being rude or abusive but confronting in a loving, spirit-led manner.

I would be remiss not to mention here in more detail the kind of people the spirit of Jezebel preys on. First and foremost, this spirit preys on people that have been wounded by ministry or some type of authority in their lives. I've seen people that were deeply wounded by a parent, spouse, elder, pastor, or spiritual leader, their trust broken, even abused. These people end up putting up emotional walls in their heart, and in a state of bitterness say, "As long as I live, I'll never again put myself under a man." Or, "Because I was hurt, I will never again submit myself to anyone else; I only need to obey God." These statements, and many others I could list, are a sure sign of the bitter fruit produced by the spirit of Jezebel. Most people I counsel and try to help who struggle with the spirit of Jezebel express the feeling they are spiritually justified in not submitting themselves. I have to work with them to gain their confidence and trust first before I can assist them in receiving deliverance.

Another bitter fruit produced by the spirit of Jezebel that goes hand in hand with unsubmission and rebellion is lawlessness. Jezebel justifies its position by discrediting any law or control preached from the Word as being "legalism" or "man's laws." They are their own authority. Principles of God's Word simply do not apply to them. The spirit of Jezebel says, "I'm special; God did not mean that for me," or, "I do not feel convicted to follow that standard or biblical principle. God supports my lack of spiritual covering because nobody has the gift like I have it, and, anyway, God deals directly with me, not through man. Nobody is anointed like me or has this special calling." That's right; they waltz in and out of assemblies saying they've heard from God or have this special "word" from God for the assembly but cannot show where they work with a covering. Jude described these "wandering stars" in verse 12, ". . . clouds *they are* without water, carried about of winds; trees whose fruit withereth, without fruit, twice dead, plucked up by the roots;"

Their ministry never produces because they have no covering. My advice to those who have been deeply wounded in their spirit by a spiritual covering, and have a hard time trusting authority because someone in authority hurt them, to pray and ask God to send a shepherd with healing hands and a heart of love to help them again value spiritual covering.

Continuing with Revelation 2:21, "And I gave her space to repent of her fornication; and she repented not."

Jezebel will not repent. This spirit scoffs and despises repentance. Jezebel may cry tears and express how much they are sorry, but there will be no change in actions or life direction. Often tears or emotions that are expressed are really a result of the humiliation they may feel at the moment from being exposed. A short time after the emotional display, this person will be right back at their same works of rebellion and unsubmission. The spirit of Jezebel aims to destroy authority and to destroy the family unit. Jezebel's main focus is her own agenda, and she will destroy the family unit if that serves her agenda. Jezebel doesn't have any concern about souls that could be lost for eternity as a result of her pervasive works. Jezebel will cry the tears, tell you she's sorry, have all the outward signs of true remorse, but in her heart there is no true change. Once the emotional outward display dies down, the same destructive patterns return again. God is not only against the spirit of Jezebel, but also the Ahab's who sit back with the authority and power to act and remove the influence of Jezebel but instead choose to do nothing.

In the home environment you can usually discern the operation of the spirit of Jezebel when husbands make statements like, "I wish I could do something about the lack of submission and honor and the display of open rebellion in my home, but you don't know my wife. Anyone who dares try to deal with her, she will make his life miserable." Of course I'm not referring to being harsh, controlling, or demanding, but the biblical role of the husband is to be the provider and spiritual protection/covering of that home. Ephesians 5:23,24 exemplifies this scriptural principle:

"²³For the husband is the head of the wife, even as Christ is the head of the church: and he is the saviour of the body. ²⁴Therefore as the church is subject unto Christ, so let the wives be to their own husbands in every thing."

As the spiritual covering, it is the duty of the husband to stand up and prevent unrighteousness entering the household or the home being adversely affected by the spirit of Jezebel operating unchecked.

Looking again at the spirit of Ahab, the apparent truth is that, rather than being the spiritual leader, Ahab simply let Jezebel have her way. I'm sure she benefited him in some way, some how, or he wouldn't have let her do the things she did.

It has been said, "The only thing that is needed for evil to reign is for good men to do nothing." Apostolic, godly men should pray, fast, and lead their homes in a way that Jezebel cannot get a toehold. There is no need to fear the spirit of Jezebel. Rather, love is the perfect antidote for the spirit of Jezebel.

1 John 4:18, "There is no fear in love. But perfect love drives out fear, because fear has to do with punishment. The man who fears is not made perfect in love." (NIV)

Apostolic men who truly serve and provide spiritual covering for their families will experience the promise of Isaiah 54:17:

"no weapon forged against you will prevail, and you will refute every tongue that accuses you. This is the heritage of the servants of the LORD, and this is their vindication from me," declares the LORD." (NIV)

This verse explains that God is not saying that weapons would not be formed and evil schemes devised and carried out against a child of God, but rather, *they would not prosper!* We must keep in mind the blessing that God gives in Revelation 2:26 to those who expose and eradicate the spirit of Jezebel:

"And he that overcometh, and keepeth my works unto the end, to him will I give power over the nations:"

The apostolic church that dares to stand up, expose, and eradicate the spirit of Jezebel, God will raise up with power to affect nations with the five-fold ministry operating within its midst. Prophetic centers will be raised up. Apostolic centers will be established as training centers for apostles, prophets, evangelists, pastors, and teachers. Jesus went on to say in Revelation 2:27,28:

"[27]And he shall rule them with a rod of iron; as the vessels of a potter shall they be broken to shivers: even as I received of my Father. [28]And I will give him the morning star."

This is an awesome promise. Anytime you see the Scripture reference the "morning star," it pertains to the Shekinah glory of God. The one thing we should all desire is to live overcoming lives immersed in the Shekinah glory of God. David made reference to this in Psalms 27:4:

"One *thing* have I desired of the LORD, that will I seek after; that I may dwell in the house of the LORD all the days of my life, to behold the beauty of the LORD, and to inquire in his temple."

The Shekinah refers to that resident habitation of the glory of God. This can only be achieved through a daily, pure, intimate relationship with Jesus Christ. A true, intimate relationship with Jesus will produce a passion for His glory. This is what Moses experienced during his pursuit of God in Exodus 33:17,18:

"*17And the LORD said unto Moses, I will do this thing also that thou hast spoken: for thou hast found grace in my sight, and I know thee by name. 18And he said, I beseech thee, shew me thy glory."* (Emphasis added)

Those who move from mere visitation of His presence to daily habitation will overcome Jezebel and will have authority to rule and operate in the anointing of the Morning Star.

When dealing with Jezebel, we must understand that Jezebel works under the cloak of a spirit in camouflage. Most of the time, Jezebel will not create a public confrontation or, for that matter, do anything openly that you can observe. Rather, Jezebel chooses to work behind the scenes with the weapons of seduction, flattery, deception, manipulation, sowing discord, disunity, strife, and confusion even orchestrating behind the scenes directly with persecution and spiritual assassination attempts. Jezebel is versed at looking you in the eye with a big smile, a handshake, or pat on the back, but, secretly in its heart, that spirit is working behind the scenes to do everything in its power, with vengeance, to destroy the man of God's credibility, influence, and authority. Only when the spirit of Jezebel is directly confronted will its true nature be revealed.

As I mentioned before, one main area Jezebel works destructively in is that of the sacred family unit. This is referenced in the book of Malachi, chapter 4, verses 5 and 6:

"5Behold, I will send you Elijah the prophet . . ."

Here the Scripture is not literally referring to Elijah physically appearing; rather, this is referring to the *spirit of Elijah*. Notice what happens when the spirit of Elijah comes:

"⁶And he shall turn the heart of the fathers to the children, and the heart of the children to their fathers, lest I come and smite the earth with a curse." (Emphasis added)

When the spirit of Elijah comes, it will bring reconciliation. Families will come together; unity will prevail. Contrarily, everything about the spirit of Jezebel destroys the family unit, defies authority of any manner, and causes division in homes, churches, and organizations. The spirit of Elijah by its very nature overthrows the works of the spirit of Jezebel.

To illustrate in one instance where the spirit of Jezebel worked, I will share a true account (names and location have been changed). Sarah moved to a church that had the same pastor for 25 years. She was directly influenced by the spirit of Jezebel. The pastor did not discern at first that this woman was being used by the enemy to influence the church in a negative manner. True to the nature of Jezebel, this woman began with flattery and subtle seduction. For the first three years she was very patient. Every chance she had, she gave gifts to the pastor and his wife and made herself readily available to serve every chance she could. She brought them gift baskets and paid for spas and other types of services that were direct personal benefits to them. In short, she simply couldn't do enough for her pastor and his wife. They were appreciative of the apparent gestures of kindness they were receiving; however, they were completely unaware of the web of deception and betrayal she was weaving.

After this woman was confident that she had gained the complete trust of the pastor and his wife, she began privately counseling key people in the church by subtly dropping statements about her "connection" and "in-road" with the pastor and his wife. These statements were designed to solidify her authenticity and apparent influence she held. Soon she began counseling saints directly against what the pastor preached and stood for. This counseling began causing division in the families and marriages. Often during counseling she would get the person to share some terrible event in their life. She would then use this as leverage against them to manipulate them. In one instance with a lady she was counseling, she used information this woman had shared about some difficulty in her marriage and a time of unfaithfulness on her part that had occurred early in her marriage to seduce this woman's husband into adultery. One day this unfortunate woman walked in on them in the act of adultery.

The woman who committed adultery blackmailed this woman by telling her, "If you tell what I did, I'm going to tell your husband and others what you told me in counseling." The spirit of Jezebel will use facts gained by trust to try to manipulate to gain the desired results. "If you tell on me, I'll tell on you."

I Kings 18:4, "For it was *so*, when Jezebel cut off the prophets of the LORD, that Obadiah took an hundred prophets, and hid them by fifty in a cave, and fed them with bread and water."

Ahab sat back on several occasions entertaining the prophet. The spirit of Ahab will sit in a service, will listen to the Word of God, and will even come up and say, "Pastor, you preached a great message." But then he will go home and do nothing about the spirit of Jezebel operating either in his life or in his household. The truth is, Ahab believed in and supported prophetic ministry as long as the prophetic words spoken supported his ideals and lifestyle (1 Kings 22:18). On the surface, it seemed Ahab genuinely supported prophetic ministry. Those influenced by the spirit of Ahab may show genuine interest in the supernatural and the operation of prophetic ministry unless that ministry confronts or exposes their lifestyle that may be contrary to the principles of the word or character of Christ. The Scriptures record in 1 Kings 21:27 of a time when Ahab was emotionally moved by the Word of the Lord:

"And it came to pass, when Ahab heard those words, that he rent his clothes, and put sackcloth upon his flesh, and fasted, and lay in sackcloth, and went softly."

Nevertheless, Ahab never dealt with Jezebel, who was involved in turning the people of Israel away from God and to Baal and other idols. When the spirit of Jezebel takes hold in a church, carnality takes over. Eventually, if Jezebel begins to influence leadership, it begins to reveal itself by presentations of immodesty. The enemy knows that most men are physically aroused to lust by sight. When a woman presents her body in an inappropriate manner by a skirt too short or tight, or a low cut blouse that is revealing, and is standing in front of a congregation singing, this causes true worship to be hindered.

As I mentioned before, if Jezebel cannot seduce you, she will try to manipulate you. If she cannot manipulate you, she will persecute you and try to destroy you. After 3½ years of drought, which was initiated by the prophetic word spoken by Elijah, God spoke to Elijah saying, ". . . Go, shew thyself unto Ahab; and I will send rain upon the earth" (1 Kings 18:1).

Elijah challenges Ahab by saying in 1 Kings 18:18,19:

"¹⁸And he answered, I have not troubled Israel; but thou, and thy father's house, in that ye have forsaken the commandments of the LORD, and thou hast followed Baalim. ¹⁹Now therefore send, and gather to me all Israel unto mount Carmel, and the prophets of Baal four hundred and fifty, and the prophets of the groves four hundred, which eat at Jezebel's table."

On Mount Carmel Elijah challenges the people by saying in 1 Kings 18:21:

". . . How long halt ye between two opinions? if the LORD be God, follow him: but if Baal, *then* follow him. And the people answered him not a word."

Elijah then sets the guidelines of this challenge in 1 Kings 18:23,24:

"²³Let them therefore give us two bullocks; and let them choose one bullock for themselves, and cut it in pieces, and lay *it* on wood, and put no fire *under*: and I will dress the other bullock, and lay it on wood, and put no fire *under*. ²⁴And call ye on the name of your gods, and I will call on the name of the LORD: and the God that answereth by fire, let him be God. And all the people answered and said, It is well spoken."

Anytime the identity of the one true God is in question within the minds of the people, God will answer by fire. The prophets of Baal chose a bullock and called upon Baal from the morning until the time of the evening sacrifice with no response.

Elijah then repaired the altar of the Lord that had been broken down. (True revival always begins with rebuilding the altars of prayer and dedication.) He then dug a trench around the altar and set the wood in order, cutting the bullock into pieces, and placing them upon the wood. He then said unto the people, "Fill four barrels with water, and pour it on the burnt sacrifice, and on the wood."

After the people obeyed, he told them to pour water on the sacrifice a second and third time until water completely filled the trench he had dug. One spiritual parallel for why Elijah did this is, when God performs a miracle, no man can receive glory or credit. If we wish to see the fire of God fall upon us in this hour, we must remove the human element from what we accomplish for God, fully trusting and depending on Him!

After a 64-word prayer, the fire fell and consumed the sacrifice, wood, stones, dust, and even the water in the trench.

1 Kings 18:39, "And when all the people saw *it*, they fell on their faces: and they said, The LORD, he is the God; the LORD, he is the God."

Elijah then called for the prophets of Baal to be destroyed. Let me pause here and say, in this hour we cannot directly attempt to fight the spirit of Jezebel for we will not win. We must leave her in the hands of God. Elijah never saw Jezebel destroyed. If a person who is under the influence of Jezebel is confronted, that person will do everything to destroy the person who confronts them. Jezebel will do whatever it takes to prove her point. In 1 Kings 21, Jezebel had Naboth killed by writing a letter in the name of Ahab just to prove a point and get his vineyard.

When Jezebel heard about her prophets being destroyed, she set her heart to destroy Elijah. Jezebel then sent a messenger, as recorded in I Kings 19:2-4:

"²Then Jezebel sent a messenger unto Elijah, saying, So let the gods do *to me*, and more also, if I make not thy life as the life of one of them by to morrow about this time."

In response to Jezebel's threat, Elijah ran. Anytime you see a man of God burnt out, discouraged, and on the run, you can be sure Jezebel is involved. Oftentimes a pastor may find himself in the middle of an attack of Jezebel. It is important that you do not try to handle this with flesh and blood methods or fight the battle in the natural. You better start praying and fasting for whomever is in authority that the spirit of Jezebel is attacking, and let God fight this battle for you.

"³And when he saw *that*, he arose, and went for his life, and came to Beersheba, which *belongeth* to Judah, and left his servant there. ⁴But he himself went a day's journey into the wilderness, and came and sat down under a juniper tree: and he requested for himself that he might die; and said, It is enough; now, O LORD, take away my life; for I *am* not better than my fathers."

Here in 1 Kings 19 we can observe the tactics Jezebel uses when she is trying to destroy a man of God. Jezebel will attempt to destroy a man of God's faith with the accusing voices of shame. Often this is accomplished by bringing up facts about your past or weaknesses in your parents, trying to convince you that "you're no better than your father was." If your father was a drunkard, you're will wind up with the same fate. Whatever the weaknesses your parents had – drugs, adultery, lying, etc. – Jezebel will attempt to humiliate you and cause you shame and to feel like you can't escape this.

During the attack that Elijah suffered, the angel came and told him, "Arise up and eat." Twice Elijah ate of the cake and drank of the cruse of water, which gave him strength for forty days of fasting. If we will be careful to daily seek the face God during our "Jezebel attacks," God will give us the strength we need for the trial.

In 1 Kings 19:9,10, we observe Elijah wallowing in self pity and the Lord's response to this:

"⁹And he came thither unto a cave, and lodged there; and, behold, the word of the LORD *came* to him, and he said unto him, What doest thou here, Elijah? ¹⁰And he said, I have been very jealous for the LORD God of hosts: for the children of Israel have forsaken thy covenant, thrown down thine altars, and slain thy prophets with the sword; and I, *even* I only, am left; and they seek my life, to take it away."

One thing we can be sure of, if we decide to throw a pity party, no one else will come (except maybe the enemy).

In 1 Kings 19:11,12, God does not respond to these words of self-pity but rather reveals to Elijah that his answer could be found in the simple intimacy of His still small voice:

"¹¹And he said, Go forth, and stand upon the mount before the LORD. And, behold, the LORD passed by, and a great and strong wind rent the mountains, and brake in pieces the rocks before the LORD; *but* the LORD was not in the wind: and after the wind an earthquake; *but* the LORD was not in the earthquake: ¹²And after the earthquake a fire; *but* the LORD *was* not in the fire: and after the fire a still small voice."

It was Elijah's personal intimacy with God that brought him out of his trial of fire. It wasn't the thundering power of the wind or the earthquake or the fire, it was a one-on-one relationship with God. Anytime a minister feels he is "burned out," he simply needs to rediscover personal intimacy with the Lord. Most people don't "backslide" overnight. It starts with losing their walk with God, their passion for prayer, and their intimacy with God. I make it a constant habit to live as an example as well as to instruct leaders in our church to seek the face of God daily. Let your daily intimacy with God falter and the enemy will start working on you. Elijah, in rediscovering his intimacy with God, it was through this intimacy that the very prophetic word that eventually brought Jezebel down was birthed.

1 Kings 19:15-19, "*15*And the LORD said unto him, Go, return on thy way to the wilderness of Damascus: and when thou comest, anoint Hazael *to be* king over Syria: *16*And Jehu the son of Nimshi shalt thou anoint *to be* king over Israel: and Elisha the son of Shaphat of Abelmeholah shalt thou anoint *to be* prophet in thy room. *17*And it shall come to pass, *that* him that escapeth the sword of Hazael shall Jehu slay: and him that escapeth from the sword of Jehu shall Elisha slay. *18*Yet I have left *me* seven thousand in Israel, all the knees which have not bowed unto Baal, and every mouth which hath not kissed him. *19*So he departed thence, and found Elisha the son of Shaphat, who *was* plowing *with* twelve yoke *of oxen* before him, and he with the twelfth: and Elijah passed by him, and cast his mantle upon him."

Out of this personal intimacy with God was birthed the spirit of Jehu, which is the spirit that eradicated Jezebel.

2 Kings 9:20-22, "*20*And the watchman told, saying, He came even unto them, and cometh not again: and the driving *is* like the driving of Jehu the son of Nimshi; for he driveth furiously. *21*And Joram said, Make ready. And his chariot was made ready. And Joram king of Israel and Ahaziah king of Judah went out, each in his chariot, and they went out against Jehu, and met him in the portion of Naboth the Jezreelite. *22*And it came to pass, when Joram saw Jehu, that he said, *Is it* peace, Jehu? And he answered, What peace,

so long as the whoredoms of thy mother Jezebel and her witchcrafts are *so* many?"

Jehu said, "I've had enough of it; I'm not putting up with it." Even when Jezebel's son comes with that same manipulative sweet-talking, "Is it peace, Jehu?," Jehu's response was, "What peace, so long as the whoredoms of thy mother Jezebel and her witchcrafts are so many?"

This is what true intercessors understand; there can be no peace as long as Jezebel is around. There are times a pastor cannot touch Jezebelic situations operating in the church. This is where the church must come through with its intercessors to rise up and pray till the stronghold is broken.

He said there's no peace – there can't be peace. Any time sin lifts its head in the church, the church wars. It's the way the church is designed, to war in prayer and fasting. The moment Jezebel saw Jehu, she first tried to seduce him:

2 Kings 9:30, "And when Jehu was come to Jezreel, Jezebel heard *of it*; and she painted her face, and tired her head, and looked out at a window."

Jehu wouldn't have anything to do with it. She didn't know whom she'd come up against. Jehu – the ministry of intercessory prayer in the church – is so vital. Pastors become weary with the battle and need intercessors to lift up their arms. Intercessors, do not be weary in well doing, keep interceding, keep travailing, keep praying. It takes time to see Jezebel defeated and, even when you defeat her, remember this is a spirit and will return to fight again if the prayer ministry falters. Almost 27 years had passed since the showdown on Mount Carmel. Immediately after the victory of Mount Carmel, Elijah struggles with spirits of depression and burnout. We find that the epic visitation of the presence of God was not found in the wind, earthquake, or fire but, rather, was discovered in the intimate, still voice of God – 1 Kings 19:15-17:

"[15]And the LORD said unto him, Go, return on thy way to the wilderness of Damascus: and when thou comest, anoint Hazael to be king over Syria: [16]And Jehu the son of Nimshi shalt thou anoint to be king over Israel: and Elisha the son of Shaphat of Abel-meholah shalt thou anoint *to be* prophet in thy room. [17]And it shall come to pass, *that* him that escapeth the sword of Hazael shall Jehu slay: and him that escapeth from the sword of Jehu shall Elisha slay."

Here Elijah, through rediscovering personal intimacy with God, anoints the three ministries who eventually brought Jezebel and all she represented down. We will win and maintain our greatest victories in life with the simple desire and passion to spend time in His presence, not for a blessing, not for a word, not for anointing, but simply because we desire to spend quality time with our King!

In all spiritual battles, you will first fight and win them on your knees in prayer before you will ever see the physical evidence of victory. We must, as spiritual warriors for our General, resist the temptation to take things into our own hands but exercise discipline to trust His Divine Hand to deal with the Jezebels in His time. The judgment wheels of God may grind painstakingly slow, but they grind thoroughly and finely and, when God is finished, He leaves no stone unturned.

Elijah anointed the ministries to deal the final deathblow to Jezebel even though he never saw her dealt with in his lifetime. This can be a very disconcerting principle for those who demand to see justice brought on Jezebel. The principle we can draw strength from is that the prayers of godly men and women never die. They still work even after the person who prayed then has passed from the scene. Pastor, if you are being worn to a frazzle trying to combat the Jezebels in your assembly, cease from warfare this instant! Rend your heart before God for the intercessory ministry of Jehu to be raised up in your assembly. Teach, train, and equip the intercessors in the flock of Christ to DAILY cover you and your family in prayer. Doing this, you will keep the intercessions that will destroy Jezebel! Pray and seek for intercessors more than finically secure saints, prominent people, or talented staff. Let the heartbeat of God found in Ezekiel 22:30 be your passionate prayer:

"And I sought for a man among them, that should make up the hedge, and stand in the gap before me for the land, . . ."

When God raises the intercessory ministry of Jehu in His church, they will be relentless. They will not flinch in the face of any demonic attack. This is represented in 2 Kings 9:31:

"And as Jehu entered in at the gate, she said, *Had* Zimri peace, who slew his master?"

Jezebel could see what was about to happen, so she shifted from seduction to manipulation (a common tactic of Jezebel). Jezebel tried to quote a biblical precedent and manipulate its true meaning to deter him from his mission. "Had Zimri peace?" No, he did not; he came to the throne by blood and deception and within seven days was constrained to burn the palace over his head and himself in it. Besides, Zimri had no warrant for what he did but was motivated by his own ambition and cruelty.

On the other hand, Jehu was anointed by God through the prophet Elijah and was on a mission from God. Jehu saw through this feeble attempt of manipulation by Jezebel.

Jehu's response is found in 2 Kings 9:32,33:

"³²And he lifted up his face to the window, and said, Who is on my side? who? And there looked out to him two or three eunuchs. ³³And he said, Throw her down. So they threw her down: and some of her blood was sprinkled on the wall, and on the horses: and he trode her under foot."

This is just how quickly God can deal with a Jezebel working havoc in a church if intercessors are trained and equipped to rise up and do "war on the floor." It has been too long that the church has turned a snidely, carnal nose up against the intercessors God raises in its midst. It has been too long that carnal ministry has lifted their hearts in human arrogance against God by attempting to perform spiritual ministry with prayerless lives. Any ministry attempt at spiritual warfare without the covering of prayer is a declaration of independence from God.

I declare that in these last days God will allow the spirit of Jezebel to be released upon the church full force to wreck havoc and destroy what has taken years to build until pastors wake up in America and realize we do need the ministry of Apostles, Prophets, Evangelists, Pastors, and Teachers (the five-fold ministry) and will recognize the tremendous value of intercessors in the church and be willing to equip and release them!

Only remember, we are not fighting against flesh and blood but a spiritual warfare. You must learn to be patient and wait on God not taking things in your own hands from a desire to "do something about Jezebel."

Fight your battles on your knees in prayer and fasting with humility. God will deal with Jezebel through the spirit of Jehu, which is intercession. This brings us to our next chapter.

Endnotes:

[i] Addis Tribune, Addis Ababa, Ethiopia March 9, 1996 section C page 2
[ii] (Biblesoft's New Exhaustive Strong's Numbers and Concordance with Expanded Greek-Hebrew Dictionary. Copyright (c) 1994, Biblesoft and International Bible Translators, Inc.)
[iii] Ibid.
[iv] Vine's Expository Dictionary of Biblical Words, Copyright (c) 1985, Thomas Nelson Publishers

2
Cultivating the Spirit of Elijah and Jehu

Revelation 2:17-21:

"^{17}He that hath an ear, let him hear what the Spirit saith unto the churches; To him that overcometh will I give to eat of the hidden manna, and will give him a white stone, and in the stone a new name written, which no man knoweth saving he that receiveth *it*. ^{18}And unto the angel of the church in Thyatira write; These things saith the Son of God, who hath his eyes like unto a flame of fire, and his feet *are* like fine brass; ^{19}I know thy works, and charity, and service, and faith, and thy patience, and thy works; and the last *to be* more than the first. ^{20}Notwithstanding I have a few things against thee, because thou sufferest that woman Jezebel, which calleth herself a prophetess, to teach and to seduce my servants to commit fornication, and to eat things sacrificed unto idols. ^{21}And I gave her space to repent of her fornication; and she repented not."

The only reason why Jezebel had power was because of the authority Ahab held as king. If Ahab had not been a wicked king of Israel, Jezebel might not have even been mentioned in the Bible. The spirit of Jezebel seeks to manipulate and to control either through indirect manipulation of authorities or by emotional blackmail.

The spirit of Jezebel often appears to be very spiritually "seasoned." This is why Jezebel is very deceptive, especially to immature Christians; when they speak or sing, you can discern the anointing of God emanating from them. *Jezebel attaches itself to those who are anointed!*

Many times the people that are afflicted by the spirit of Jezebel are good people reacting to bad situations. Leadership must be cautious in dealing with those influenced by Jezebel.

A "mishandled" person under the influence of Jezebel can do much damage to the work of God. The best thing to do is to handle these people with love, patience, and compassion and let the ministry of intercessors cover with prayer.

We are at war with the spirits of this age, not the people! We can cast down the strongholds of the enemy while saving the souls of men. Eventually God will deal with these people by either bringing them to repentance or removing them, and you will not have to get your hands "bloody."

We must be careful and cautious in our spirit when we do experience wounding from these people that we don't become prey to the spirit of Jezebel ourselves. If you've been wounded by ministry or authority, whether it is a father, mother, a pastor, or others, you must take those wounds to God.

In Luke chapter 15 parable of the prodigal son, the prodigal apparently allowed the difficulty he suffered with the elder brother to cause him to separate himself from his relationship with his father. We need to let those wounds we may suffer from our brethren become grief before God, not a broken relationship with Him. He will cleanse our spirit from emotions of bitterness and anger, but we've got to choose to submit ourselves to the working of His hand.

One principle in the spirit realm is, the way to defeat the influence and operation of demonic spirits is to do the exact opposite of what that spirit is trying to work in you. If it's rebellion, then submit yourself. If it's arrogance, then humble yourself. If it's pride, you choose meekness. When you choose the exact opposite of what the spirit is that comes against you, eventually, with prayer and fasting, you defeat it.

Ministers of God must be careful to always remain submitted to the covering God has placed over them. Most people that have the spirit of Jezebel are only in authority to themselves. They're not subject to anybody. They may say they're in subjection, but they're really not. There is nobody in their lives empowered to speak a word of correction to them a word of balance. Even if they become accountable or submit themselves to somebody, they start switching the people they're accountable to if that person does not see it their way or counsel them "according to their desires."

I have pastored saints that always compared my counsel to a "second opinion" from some "prayer covering" or "spiritual covering" many states away. This results in people who jump from church to church and place to place like tumble weeds blowing in the wind. Everything is wonderful during the "honeymoon stage" of attending a church until that pastor gets down where they live and starts pastoring them, not just taking their tithes, but sitting down and asking the hard questions and finding out where they "live" and expecting them to "grow up."

This is why Paul instructed the Ephesian Church in Ephesians 4:14,15:

"[14]That we *henceforth* be no more children, tossed to and fro, and carried about with every wind of doctrine, by the sleight of men, and cunning craftiness, whereby they lie in wait to deceive; [15]But *speaking the truth in love, may grow up into him in all things*, which is the head, *even* Christ:" (Emphasis added)

One of the most difficult things I have discovered in serving as a pastor is to get saints to act their age. Most adults want to throw a tantrum and act like 10-year-olds.

Most saints that are overcome by Jezebel will not endure correction from a pastor. 1 Kings 18:16,17 records that Ahab did not view himself as being the problem, but Elijah:

"[16]So Obadiah went to meet Ahab and told him, and Ahab went to meet Elijah. [17]When he saw Elijah, he said to him, "Is that you, you troubler of Israel?" [i]

The Scriptures also record in Proverbs 12:1 and 15:10:

"Whoever loves discipline loves knowledge, but he who hates correction is stupid.[ii]

"Correction *is* grievous unto him that forsaketh the way: *and* he that hateth reproof shall die."

When a person influenced by Jezebel is corrected and will not receive it or repent, they then use false spirituality to produce a "word" either given by an external authority or in supposed prayer that "calls" them to a different church or city. Then, like tumbleweeds with no roots, they bounce from place to place until they find a pastor who will leave them alone and let them be an authority to themselves.

Often these rebellious saints, carried away with this deception, call themselves to be a pastor so they do not have to submit to anyone. (The truth is, all pastors, evangelists, prophets, apostles, and teachers must always be accountable to someone and under a covering of authority.)

Without submission to authority, we cannot have true spiritual authority with God. This spiritual principle is reflected in the scriptural account found in Luke 7:6-9:

"6Then Jesus went with them. And when he was now not far from the house, the centurion sent friends to him, saying unto him, Lord, trouble not thyself: for I am not worthy that thou shouldest enter under my roof: 7Wherefore neither thought I myself worthy to come unto thee: but say in a word, and my servant shall be healed. 8For I also am a man set under authority, having under me soldiers, and I say unto one, Go, and he goeth; and to another, Come, and he cometh; and to my servant, Do this, and he doeth it. 9When Jesus heard these things, he marvelled at him, and turned him about, and said unto the people that followed him, I say unto you, *I have not found so great faith, no, not in Israel.*" (Emphasis added)

I believe this great faith the centurion possessed was a result of his understanding of authority.

People who struggle with rebellion can only find victory when they choose to submit their lives under the covering God has given them. Even after Jezebel has been conquered, it takes time to teach and retrain the human spirit that has learned habits that were the fruit of Jezebel's operation in their life. When somebody says, "I think this certain person has a demonic spirit influencing them," I say, "Great! We can deal with that! We can fast and pray, and we will conquer this spirit." It's in dealing with the human spirit where the trouble is. We cannot "conquer" a human spirit; we must teach the human spirit.

Many ministries become frustrated, controlling, and even abusive because they try to conquer the human spirit of man. We cannot cast out a human spirit either, for, if we do, we are going to go to jail for murder! You've got to *teach* human spirits. Once you break the spirit of Jezebel, and the spirit's influence is gone, there's still fruit of learned activity and learned responses that have got to be dealt with through teaching. If the person who has experienced deliverance from the influence of Jezebel is not immediately and carefully taught scriptural knowledge, then Jezebel might return with a vengeance.

This principle is found in Luke 11:24-26:

"24When the unclean spirit is gone out of a man, he walketh through dry places, seeking rest; and finding none, he saith, I will return unto my house whence I came out. 25And when he cometh, he findeth it swept and garnished. 26Then goeth he, and taketh *to him* seven other spirits more wicked than himself; and they enter in, and dwell there: and the last *state* of that man is worse than the first."

When you conquer Jezebel through effectual, fervent prayer, you've got to hang a sign on your heart that says, "No Vacancy." How? We accomplish this through continually applying obedience to the teaching and principles of the Word and daily dying to the flesh. It goes without saying that we must choose to allow our lives to be filled to overflowing with the power of the Spirit.

This is why Paul wrote in 1 Corinthians 9:27:

"But I keep under my body, and bring it into subjection: lest that by any means, when I have preached to others, I myself should be a castaway."

We must not become spiritual castaways. Without true repentance, scriptural teaching to adjust our human responses, and being daily filled with the Holy Spirit's anointing, Jezebel can return and bring many other spirits with it. (Remember, the spirit of Jezebel is a stronghold spirit, which means it is a spirit that rules and brings many other spirits with it.)

Resist the temptation of human response to constantly argue, battle, confront, and challenge what the spiritual covering in your life says, but, rather, submit yourself to the Word and to the covering God has given you.

This is most easily done as an intercessor given to daily prayer and fasting. I have observed very few true intercessors in the spirit that were proud and uncommitted. This is why intercessors must first establish the foundation of consistency in personal intimacy with Christ. Anyone who attempts to be an intercessor without an established relationship with God falls prey to Jezebel.

As a matter of fact, most people who try to be intercessors in prayer warfare without first developing a deep daily intimacy with God eventually lose out altogether. Intimacy is the true spirit of intercession. We gain a foundation of intimacy with Christ by daily commitment to spiritual communion and abiding in Him. Daily abiding in Him allows the fruit and gifts of the Spirit to develop in our lives to full maturity!

John 15:4, "Abide in me, and I in you. As the branch cannot bear fruit of itself, except it abide in the vine; no more can ye, except ye abide in me."

True success in the Kingdom of God is produced by daily abiding in Him. Any ministry or gift operation that is not born out of our intimacy with Christ will ultimately result in being an unfruitful ministry. Everything about the spirit of intercession – the spirit of Jehu – ties in with what Jesus spoke in John 7:37,38:

"37On the last day, that great *day* of the feast, Jesus stood and cried out, saying, "If anyone thirsts, let him come to Me and drink. 38He who believes in Me, as the Scripture has said, out of his heart will flow rivers of living water." (NKJV)

To become a true Jehu, you must ask yourself two questions. The first question is, am I part of the flow of the river or am I on the bank?

This question stems from the account found recorded in Ezekiel 47:1-12:

"1Afterward he brought me again unto the door of the house; and, behold, waters issued out from under the threshold of the house eastward: for the forefront of the house *stood toward* the east, and the waters came down from under from the right side of the house, at the south *side* of the altar. 2Then brought he me out of the way of the gate northward, and led me about the way without unto the utter gate by the way that looketh eastward; and, behold, there ran out waters on the right side. 3And when the man that had the line in his hand went forth eastward, he measured a thousand cubits, and he brought me through the waters; the waters *were* to the ankles. 4Again he measured a thousand, and brought me through the waters; the waters *were* to the knees. Again he measured a thousand, and brought me through; the waters *were* to the loins. ⁵Afterward he measured a thousand; *and it was* a river that I could not pass over: for the waters were risen, waters to swim in, a river that could not be passed over.

"⁶And he said unto me, Son of man, hast thou seen *this?* Then he brought me, and caused me to return to the brink of the river. ⁷Now when I had returned, behold, at the bank of the river *were* very many trees on the one side and on the other. ⁸Then said he unto me, These waters issue out toward the east country, and go down into the desert, and go into the sea: *which being* brought forth into the sea, the waters shall be healed. ⁹And it shall come to pass, *that* every thing that liveth, which moveth, whithersoever the rivers shall come, shall live: and there shall be a very great multitude of fish, because these waters shall come thither: for they shall be healed; and every thing shall live whither the river cometh.

¹⁰And it shall come to pass, *that* the fishers shall stand upon it from En-gedi even unto En-eglaim; they shall be a *place* to spread forth nets; their fish shall be according to their kinds, as the fish of the great sea, exceeding many. ¹¹But the miry places thereof and the marishes thereof shall not be healed; they shall be given to salt. ¹²And by the river upon the bank thereof, on this side and on that side, shall grow all trees for meat, whose leaf shall not fade, neither shall the fruit thereof be consumed: it shall bring forth new fruit according to his months, because their waters they issued out of the sanctuary: and the fruit thereof shall be for meat, and the leaf thereof for medicine."

Ezekiel did not discover the healing power in the waters until he was in waters to swim in. Ankle deep, knee deep, and even waters to the loins still allowed Ezekiel to stand on the bank of the river (the river bottom was simply an extension of the bank) and ultimately control his direction and destiny. When Ezekiel enters "waters to swim in," he was no longer in complete control, but, rather, the river carried him.

When we are able to create a spiritual environment where the Holy Spirit moves as rivers of living water, then we will become true anointed assemblies of healing, miracles, and deliverance! These healing places of ministry will see the ingathering of multitudes of fish (people).

Those assemblies that do not seek for the deep waters of the Spirit will be in miry places (islands unto themselves) and marshes (stagnant, shallow waters) and will be given to salt (unable to sustain life).

One example of this is the Dead Sea in Israel, which has such a high salt content that it cannot sustain animal or plant life. Its banks are desolate and empty. What a contrast to the church that has living waters flowing through it! These churches have trees for meat (true, deep, spiritual ministry), leaves that never fade (consistent, vibrant ministries), and are constantly bringing forth new fruit (ministries) in its seasons.

The second question you should ask yourself is, am I a bucket or a conduit? This question stems from the account found in Zechariah 4:1-6:

"¹And the angel that talked with me came again, and waked me, as a man that is wakened out of his sleep, ²And said unto me, What seest thou? And I said, I have looked, and behold a candlestick all *of* gold, with a bowl upon the top of it, and his seven lamps thereon, and seven pipes to the seven lamps, which *are* upon the top thereof: ³And two olive trees by it, one upon the right *side* of the bowl, and the other upon the left *side* thereof. ⁴So I answered and spake to the angel that talked with me, saying, What *are* these, my lord? ⁵Then the angel that talked with me answered and said unto me, Knowest thou not what these be? And I said, No, my lord. ⁶Then he answered and spake unto me, saying, This is the word of the LORD unto Zerubbabel, saying, Not by might, nor by power, but by my spirit, saith the LORD of hosts."

In the Old Testament, one of the daily duties of the priest was to make sure he lamp in the temple never burned out (see Exodus 27:20). This required the priest to daily refill the lamp with olive oil. This vision depicts the hour when we (the lamps) would be connected directly to the source of oil or the olive trees (daily being filled with the Holy Spirit by walking in intimacy of prayer) thus not depending on might or power in the flesh but being daily directed and empowered by the Holy Spirit. We must stay connected daily to our true source of power, the Holy Spirit, and ever seek to walk as led of His Spirit. When we choose to have a "bucket" mentality, we will only seek to give out if we feel we have virtue in our bucket.

All too often, events in life put holes in our bucket and what virtue we feel we may have left is gone. If we will change our mentality from "fill my cup, Lord" to "Lord, I want to be a conduit for your virtue to flow through," then we will be more effective ministers. When we are connected to the source (Jesus), His virtue is a never-ending supply.

A pastor would be wise to build an army of dedicated intercessors to cover him daily in prayer. In the heat of the battle with Jezebel, the spirit of Jehu can rise up and defeat Jezebel time and time again.

Taking time to raise intercessors within a congregation is more important to true apostolic growth than any building program, outreach program, event, or church function. The battle cry of Jehu in the modern church should be as according to Isaiah 62:1,2:

"¹For Zion's sake I will not keep silent, for Jerusalem's sake I will not remain quiet, till her righteousness shines out like the dawn, her salvation like a blazing torch. ²The nations will see your righteousness, and all kings your glory; you will be called by a new name that the mouth of the LORD will bestow."[iii]

And Isaiah 62:6,7:

"⁶I have set watchmen upon thy walls, O Jerusalem, *which* shall never hold their peace day nor night: ye that make mention of the LORD, keep not silence, ⁷And give him no rest, till he establish, and till he make Jerusalem a praise in the earth."

Intercessors, keep not silent, lift up your voices for victory in this warfare. The church that has equipped persistent intercessors is the church that will experience continual revival and growth.

This chosen path of intercessory prayer can be found illustrated in Job 28:7,8:

"⁷*There is* a path which no fowl knoweth, and which the vulture's eye hath not seen: ⁸The lion's whelps have not trodden it, nor the fierce lion passed by it."

This verse speaks of the path of intercessory prayer. Vultures are known to first peck at the eyes of wounded prey knowing that, if they can destroy the vision, they can eventually consume the whole body. There are spiritual vultures that seek to rob the church of its vision.

On this path of prayer, according to Job 28:7,8, the vulture's eye has not even seen it. The lion's whelps (speaking of those new temptations that try to catch you unaware) have not trodden this path of prayer. The fierce lion (speaking of that familiar trial that tries to snare you) has not passed by it. It is truly on the path of intercessory prayer that the wicked one "cannot even touch us."

I recall in the summer of 1992 while I was ministering in London, England, I had a dream. In this dream I was surrounded by dwarf demons. They were all about 2-3 feet tall, and they were trying to torment me. In this dream I looked to the side and saw a small path leading to a higher place. In a few steps I was on this path and a few feet above the dwarf imps. I was surprised when they tried to get to me but could not. They could not see the path! I can still remember them jumping angrily trying to reach me but were unable to. I awoke to the voice of the Spirit prompting me that this dream represented the path of prayer and what really happens when one enters into intimacy with God through prayer.

There is such a path, and that path is prayer. Prayer is the path upon which you can walk and the enemy cannot even reach you. The Bible tells us in I John 5:18:

"We know that whosoever is born of God sinneth not; but he that is begotten of God keepeth himself, and *that wicked one toucheth him not."* (Emphasis added)

It is the path we can walk — a path we can climb as an eagle into the heights of the supernatural and deep things of God. We will be remembered in this life only for our passions. We must choose to have passion in prayer! Jesus prayed with strong crying.

Hebrews 5:7, "Who in the days of his flesh, when he had offered up prayers and supplications with strong crying and tears unto him that was able to save him from death, and was heard in that he feared;"

As prayer warriors committed to the spirit of Jehu, we must have our "certain times" of prayer as in Luke 11:1:

"And it came to pass, that, as he was praying in a certain place, when he ceased, one of his disciples said unto him, Lord, teach us to pray, as John also taught his disciples."

And Luke 6:12, "And it came to pass in those days, that he went out into a mountain to pray, and continued all night in prayer to God."

We must also learn to live in the spirit of prayer according to 1 Thessalonians 5:17:

"Pray without ceasing."

That is, keep in a spirit of prayer no matter where you are throughout the day. Pray in your spirit while driving, working, and playing, etc., remaining ever sensitive to the call of God to prayer! (See Luke 11:1 above)

Psalms 84:3 should be the goal of every intercessor:

"Yea, the sparrow hath found an house, and the swallow a nest for herself, where she may lay her young, *even* thine altars, O LORD of hosts, my King, and my God."

Rather than spinning our wheels trying to gain political advantage against Jezebel, or any physical position of advantage, or following the latest fad of "prayer," we should seek the face of God trusting Psalms 34:18:

"The LORD *is* nigh unto them that are of a broken heart; and saveth such as be of a contrite spirit."

The most strategic place we can pray is not the highest position in an area but the lowest position in our hearts of brokenness and hunger. "The secret of the Lord *is* with them that fear him; and he will shew them his covenant" (Psalm 25:14). Messages are not born in the study but rather on our knees in prayer. Burdens are released on our knees in prayer. Sins are remitted on our knees in prayer. Evil imaginations are captured on our knees in prayer. Doubts and fear are expelled on our knees in prayer. Strongholds are broken on our knees in prayer. Families are made stronger on our knees in prayer. Churches grow stronger on our knees in prayer. We become a stronger nation on our knees in prayer. *Our most influential position in God's kingdom is on our knees in prayer!*

Some things come not out but by *prayer and fasting!*

We must become skilled in waging war against the spirit of Jezebel. The spirit of Elijah (true apostolic pastors and prophets) and the spirit of Jehu (apostolic intercessory prayer ministry) are given to the church by God in this End Time to wage this warfare. We will discuss in chapter three more details on how to defeat Jezebel, but I want to discuss the importance of the five-fold ministry to the church and, in particular, the anointed office of the prophet in relation to Jezebel.

The five-fold ministry can be likened to the hand of God. The apostle is the thumb, the prophet the index finger, the evangelist the middle finger, the pastor the ring finger, and the teacher the pinky.

God is restoring His Apostolic Church in this hour. This restoration is according to the prophecy of the prophet Joel in Joel 2:23-29:

"23Be glad then, ye children of Zion, and rejoice in the LORD your God: for he hath given you the former rain moderately, and he will cause to come down for you the rain, the former rain, and the latter rain in the first *month.* ²⁴And the floors shall be full of wheat, and the fats shall overflow with wine and oil. ²⁵And I will restore to you the years that the locust hath eaten, the cankerworm, and the caterpiller, and the palmerworm, my great army which I sent among you. ²⁶And ye shall eat in plenty, and be satisfied, and praise the name of the LORD your God, that hath dealt wondrously with you: and my people shall never be ashamed. ²⁷And ye shall know that I *am* in the midst of Israel, and *that* I *am* the LORD your God, and none else: and my people shall never be ashamed.

²⁸And it shall come to pass afterward, *that* I will pour out my spirit upon all flesh; and your sons and your daughters shall prophesy, your old men shall dream dreams, your young men shall see visions: ²⁹And also upon the servants and upon the handmaids in those days will I pour out my spirit."

The word 'restore' has the meaning make amends, (make an) end, finish, full, give again, make good, (re-)pay (again), (make) (to) (be at) peace(-able), that is perfect, perform, (make) prosper(-ous), recompense, render, requite, make restitution, restore, reward, surely.[iv]

In this hour we are witnessing the final restoration of the Apostolic Church.

One main area of the Apostolic Church that God is restoring is the five-fold ministry. The five-fold ministry is actually an extension of God's hand working in His body the Church. To quote Lee Stoneking: "The Apostle *governs*, the Prophet *guides*, the Evangelist *gathers*, the Pastor *guards*, the Teacher *grounds*." The Apostle Paul writes concerning the five-fold ministry in Ephesians 4:7-11:

"⁷But unto every one of us is given grace according to the measure of the gift of Christ. ⁸Wherefore he saith, When he ascended up on high, he led captivity captive, and gave gifts unto men. ⁹(Now that he ascended, what is it but that he also descended first into the lower parts of the earth? ¹⁰He that descended is the same also that ascended up far above all heavens, that he might fill all things.) ¹¹And he gave some, **apostles**; and some, **prophets**; and some, **evangelists**; and some, **pastors** and **teachers**; ¹²For the perfecting of the saints, for the work of the ministry, for the edifying of the body of Christ:" (Emphasis added)

The word 'apostle' in these verses is translated from the Greek word *apostolos* {ap-os'-tol-os} which has the following meaning: apostolos (ap-os'-tol-os) NT:652; from NT:649; a delegate; specially, an ambassador of the Gospel; officially a commissioner of Christ ["apostle"] (with miraculous powers): KJV – apostle, messenger, *he that is sent.*ᵛ

The word 'prophet' in these verses is translated from the Greek word *prophetes* {prof-ay-tace} which can have the following meanings:

1) In Greek writings, an interpreter of oracles or of other hidden things.

2) One who, moved by the Spirit of God and hence his organ or spokesman, solemnly declares to men what he has received by inspiration, especially concerning future events and, in particular, such as relate to the cause and kingdom of God and to human salvation.
    2a) The OT prophets having foretold the kingdom, deeds, and death of Jesus the Messiah
    2b) Of John the Baptist the herald of Jesus the Messiah
    2c) Of the illustrious prophet the Jews expected before the advent of the Messiah

2d) The Messiah
2e) Of men filled with the Spirit of God who, by God's authority and command in words of weight, plead the cause of God and urge the salvation of men
2f) Of prophets that appeared in the Apostolic Age among Christians
2f1) They are associated with the apostles
2f2) They discerned and did what is best for the Christian cause, foretelling certain future events (see Acts 11:27)

3) A poet (because poets were believed to sing under divine inspiration)[vi]

The word 'evangelist' in these verses is translated from the Greek word *euaggelistes* {yoo-ang-ghel-is-tace'} which has the following meanings:

1) A bringer of good tidings, an evangelist

2) The name given to the NT heralds of salvation through Christ who are not apostles [vii]

The word 'pastors' in these verses is translated from the Greek word *poimen* {poy-mane'} which can have the following meanings:

1) A herdsman, especially a shepherd
1a) In the parable, he to whose care and control others have committed themselves, and whose precepts they follow

2) Metaph
2a) The presiding officer, manager, director of any assembly: so of Christ the Head of the church
2a1) Of the overseers of the Christian assemblies
2a2) Of kings and princes [viii]

The word 'teachers' in these verses is translated from the Greek word didaskalos {did-as-kal-os}, which can have the following meanings:

1) A teacher
2) In the NT one who teaches concerning the things of God and the duties of man
    2a) One who is fitted to teach or thinks himself so
    2b) The teachers of the Jewish religion
    2c) Of those who by their great power as teachers draw crowds around them, i.e. John the Baptist, Jesus
    2d) By preeminence used of Jesus by Himself, as one who showed men the way of salvation
    2e) Of the apostles and of Paul
    2f) Of those who in the religious assemblies of the Christians undertook the work of teaching with the special assistance of the Holy Spirit
    2g) Of false teachers among Christians [ix]

Some theologians erroneously teach that the ministry of the apostle and prophet was only for the establishing of the Scriptures and the original church. This error is not supported by biblical or historical facts.

In the First Church we can observe the full function of the five-fold ministry in operation. This is seen scattered throughout the book of the Acts of the Apostles and through the letters written during the first 75 years of the church's existence. Each part of the five-fold ministry is not necessarily a position of power but an office of ministry or function. It is apparent in the Scriptures that one person could operate in more than one function though one particular ministry will tend to be a primary.

We can see in the Scriptures that each function of the five-fold ministry is intermittently exchangeable in ministry operation. I have come to recognize that I function primarily as a prophet; secondarily I operate most effectively in administration and evangelism. It is by God's grace and enablement that I have operated as a pastor for the past eight years, but this is mostly through a staff that has pastoral gifts.

Let us look at each particular function of the five-fold ministry in relation to biblical characters and the hand of God.

Just as a human hand has five fingers, the five-fold ministry as the hand of God also has five fingers (functions).

Paul and Peter the Apostles (the thumb of God)

The apostle can be likened to the thumb on the hand. The thumb is the one finger that is in constant contact with all the other fingers, thus it is the apostle who networks in constant contact with all the others of the five-fold ministry. The apostle is often considered a minister to the ministers, a preacher to the preachers, a spiritual father, and a leader of men of God. A few of the apostle's functions are to govern, pioneer, and be a father and mentor to younger ministers. When God wants to bring a city, region, or nation renewal and harvest, He sends an apostle.

Mark 16:15, "And he said unto them, Go ye into all the world, and preach the gospel to every creature."

The basic definition of the word 'apostle' is *"sent ones."* It is taken from the Greek word (NT:652) *apostolos* (ap-os'-tol-os), from NT:649 a delegate, specially an ambassador of the Gospel, officially a commissioner of Christ ["apostle"] (with miraculous powers): KJV – apostle, messenger, he that is sent. [x]

Before this was a biblical word, it was a secular term used by Greeks and Romans to describe special envoys who were sent out for the purpose of expanding the dominion of the empire. Many of these envoys were military generals with authority to go into new territories and fight, if necessary, to establish the Greek or Roman culture in that region. They were also responsible for teaching and training the new subjects in the laws and culture of the kingdom.

These envoys were given power and authority from the king to fulfill their mission. They were responsible for fulfilling their commissions and were given everything needed to succeed. They were sent to certain territories and charged to subdue, conquer, convert, instruct, train, and establish the new subjects in the culture of the empire. Apostles are the spiritual commanders or generals of the church. The apostle's mantle includes warfare strategy and rulership.

Isaiah 55:4, "Behold, I have given him for a witness to the people, a leader and commander to the people."

The Hebrew word 'commander,' as used in Isaiah 55:4, is the Hebrew word (OT:6680) *tsavah* (tsaw-vaw'); a primitive root; (intensively) to constitute, enjoin: KJV – appoint, (for-)bid, (give a) charge, (give a, give in, send with) command(-er, -ment), send a messenger, put, (set) in order. The Church needs apostolic leadership to help set the Church in order. Apostles are standard-bearers-commanders who lift the standard and rally the army of God (see Isaiah 59:19). Apostles have the ability as generals and commanders to mobilize the saints for war. As an officer in the Church, the apostle is also an executive. He is a person who executes power in the Church. In other words, he has the power and authority to execute the plans and purposes of God. To execute means to put into effect, to carry out, to perform, to fulfill, to finish. The purposes of God will not be fulfilled or carried out without the apostolic ministry being restored to the Church.

Although every believer has rank to cast out devils, apostles walk and minister in the highest rank. Evil spirits and angels recognize this rank.

The word 'apostle' has been a part of the Church since the days our Lord ministered on the Earth. It now describes the commission given to the first apostles. They were sent into the territories of the Earth to convert multitudes of people and incorporate them into the Kingdom of God. They were given power and authority to accomplish the task. They were responsible for teaching, training, and instructing the new believers, making them productive citizens of the Kingdom. Apostles were sent to establish the Kingdom in the hearts of people and to establish churches throughout the world. They were given the power of the Holy Spirit to help them fulfill this mission.

If the commission is apostolic, that means only sent ones can fulfill it. It is the responsibility of the apostles to release and stir up the apostolic dimension in every believer through teaching, preaching, prophesying, and the laying on of hands. [xi]

This will do more to deal a deathblow to Jezebel than anything else. The following Scripture references are pertaining to Paul being an apostle:

Galatians 1:1, "Paul, an apostle (not from men nor through man, but through Jesus Christ and God the Father who raised Him from the dead)," (NKJV)

Ephesians 2:20,21, "[20]And are built upon the foundation of the apostles and prophets, Jesus Christ himself being the chief corner *stone;* [21]In whom all the building fitly framed together groweth unto an holy temple in the Lord:"

2 Corinthians 12:11,12, "¹¹I am become a fool in glorying; ye have compelled me: for I ought to have been commended of you: for in nothing am I behind the very chiefest apostles, though I be nothing. ¹²Truly the signs of an apostle were wrought among you in all patience, in signs, and wonders, and mighty deeds."

Although the primary office/ministry of Paul was recognized as being an apostle, he also operated in other ministries.

2 Timothy 1:11, "Whereunto I am appointed a *preacher*, and an *apostle*, and a *teacher* of the Gentiles." (Emphasis added)

Peter was also considered an apostle and was named as an apostle in the second epistle which bears his name:

2 Peter 1:1, "Simon Peter, a bondservant and apostle of Jesus Christ, To those who have obtained like precious faith with us by the righteousness of our God and Savior Jesus Christ:" (NKJV)

It is interesting to note that the date of the writing of the second chapter of Peter is approximately 30 years after the establishing of the First Church, thus refuting the claim that apostles were only for the establishing of the church. Two references in 2 Peter give some indication of the date of the epistle. In 2 Peter 1:13-15, Peter indicated that the time of his death was near. The traditional date for Peter's death is late AD 67 or early AD 68. The reference to Paul's epistles in 3:16 would seem to indicate a date some time after AD 60. Since 1 Peter is normally dated around AD 64, 2 Peter may be conservatively placed some time after the writing of 1 Peter and before Peter's death, between AD 64 and 68.[xii]

The spirit of Elijah can be exercised by the apostle, prophet, and pastor. While we are referencing the office of the apostle, I will make some observations of the apostle in regard to the spirit of Jezebel.

Apostles in the apostolic church will be closely acquainted with spiritual warfare.

2 Corinthians 10:4,5, "⁴For the weapons of our warfare *are* not carnal but mighty in God for pulling down strongholds, ⁵casting down arguments and every high thing that exalts itself against the knowledge of God, bringing every thought into captivity to the obedience of Christ,"[xiii]

'Warfare' in this verse is translated from the Greek word *strateia* (strat-i'-ah) NT:4752; from NT:4754; military service, i.e. (figuratively) the apostolic career (as one of hardship and danger): KJV – warfare.[xiv] It is related to the Greek word *strateuomai*, meaning to execute the apostolate (with its arduous duties and functions) and to contend with carnal thoughts.

There are many strongholds that cannot be destroyed without a true apostolic anointing from God. 'Stronghold' is the Greek word *ochuroma* (okh-oo'-ro-mah) NT:3794; from a remote derivative of NT:2192 (meaning to fortify, through the idea of holding safely); a castle (figuratively, argument): KJV – stronghold.[xv]

The enemy has fortified themselves and built strongholds against invasion. They have built strongholds and fortified themselves in every region of the world to resist the advancement of the Kingdom. These strongholds must be dealt with if we are to see the fulfillment of the Great Commission. Apostles have the ability to confront and pull down these strongholds.

The Apostle Paul links these strongholds with 'imaginations.' This is the Greek word *logismos,* meaning reasoning, thought computation, or logic. It carries the idea of holding something safely. It is simply the way people think based on their way of life, tradition, experience, or past teaching. Unfortunately, most thinking is against the knowledge of God. The stronghold is also made up of demonic influence. There is a wisdom that is earthly, sensual, and devilish (see James 3:15).

Logismos can also be translated as 'arguments.' Strongholds are the mind-sets of people in a particular territory. These mind-sets are fortified places that keep out truth and hold in lies. Unbelievers have mind-sets that prevent them from receiving the truth of the Gospel. Spiritual warfare involves demolishing these mind-sets so that people can receive and walk in the truth. Strongholds do two things: They keep people from the knowledge of God, and they prevent people from obeying the truth. Ignorance and rebellion are the result. The term *mind-set* depicts a combination of both mind and set. In other words, the mind is already settled on a set of beliefs and therefore resistant to change. This means it is fixed and rigid.

Mind-sets are the thought processes of groups of people who have developed a way of thinking over centuries of time. It is a combination of their experiences and what they have been taught by their ancestors. Mind-sets are not easy to change. It takes a strong anointing to break through the defensive barriers in their minds and overcome the pride associated with their way of thinking.

These strongholds are so strong that they are likened to forts. A fort is a citadel, a garrison, a castle, a tower, or a safeguard. We have all heard the saying "hold the fort!" It means to defend and maintain the status quo. People would rather maintain their present way of thinking than to change. They will defend the current way of thinking through argument and debate. They will contradict and even blaspheme if necessary.

Communism is a mind-set; it is an ideology and a philosophy of life. Materialism is a mind-set that bases happiness on success. Humanism is a mind-set. Poverty is (in some cases) a mind-set. Islam is a mind-set. Hinduism is a mind-set. These philosophies control the minds of countless people. These are powerful strongholds that can only be overcome through apostolic preaching and teaching.

Strongholds are major hindrances to the advancement of the Church and must be dealt with apostolically. The preaching, teaching, and overall ministry of apostolic people are weapons that are mighty through God for the pulling down of these strongholds. (Praise, worship, fasting, and prayer are also effective weapons.) The first thing Jesus gave the Twelve when He sent them forth was power over devils (see Matthew 10:1).

The Church must have the ability to blast and demolish these fortresses. Apostolic ministry has the power and authority to destroy strongholds and change mind-sets. There is a grace, a supernatural ability to refute, disprove, discredit, and expose these philosophies for what they are. People will not repent unless there is a change of mind. This is the warfare that the Apostle Paul is referring to in 2 Corinthians 10:3-5 refuting arguments and taking captive philosophies that are contrary to the truth.[xvi]

Agabus the Prophet (the index finger of God)

The prophet can be likened to the index finger that often points the way. The prophet, through direct words from God and through other manners, "points" the way to God's will and purpose. The word 'prophet' comes from the Greek word (NT:4396) *prophetes* (prof-ay'-tace); from a compound of NT:4253 and NT:5346; a foreteller ("prophet"); by analogy, an inspired speaker; by extension, a poet: KJV – prophet.[xvii]

The prophet reveals the heart of man and the purpose of God according to the Word of God. The prophet shares in the secrets of God.

Amos 3:7, "Surely the Lord GOD does nothing, *Unless He reveals His secret* to His servants the prophets." (NKJV) (Emphasis added)

In the operation of the First Church in the book of Acts, they were moved by the Holy Spirit to speak having power to instruct, comfort, encourage, rebuke, convict, and stimulate those who heard them.

We first discover mention of Agabus the Prophet in Acts 11:27,28:

"[27]And in these days prophets came from Jerusalem to Antioch. [28]Then one of them, named Agabus, stood up and showed by the Spirit that there was going to be a great famine throughout all the world, which also happened in the days of Claudius Caesar." (NKJV)

While some may claim that the ministries of the prophet and apostle were only for the establishing of the Church and does not operate in this time, the Scriptures bear record differently. In the operation of Agabus, we find this ministry of the prophet alive and well many years after the First Church was started.

Acts 13:1 not only supports the fact that the ministries of the prophet and teacher were alive and well, but also suggests that prophets can also abide in the ministry of a teacher. (See also Ephesians 3:4-5; 1 Timothy 1:8-9.)

Now in the church that was at Antioch there were certain prophets and teachers: Barnabas, Simeon who was called Niger, Lucius of Cyrene, Manaen who had been brought up with Herod the Tetrarch, and Saul.

The following list is a few examples with references to the prophet's place in Old and New Testament Scripture.

1. God spoke of old by – Hosea 12:10; Hebrews 1:1
2. The messengers of God – 2 Chronicles 36:15; Isaiah 44:26
3. The servants of God – Jeremiah 35:15
4. The watchmen of Israel – Ezekiel 3:17
5. Were called:
    a. Men of God – 1 Samuel 9:6
    b. Prophets of God – Ezra 5:2
    c. Holy prophets – Luke 1:70; Revelation 18:20; 22:6
    d. Holy men of God – 2 Peter 1:21
    e. Seers – 1 Samuel 9:9
6. Were esteemed as holy men – 2 Kings 4:9
7. Women sometimes endowed as – Joel 2:28
8. God communicated to:
    a. His secret things – Amos 3:7
    b. At various times and in different ways – Hebrews 1:1
    c. By an audible voice – Numbers 12:8; 1 Samuel 3:4-14
    d. By angels – Daniel 8:15-26; Revelation 22:8,9
    e. By dreams and visions – Numbers 12:6; Joel 2:28
9. Were under the influence of the Holy Spirit while prophesying – Luke 1:67; 2 Peter 1:21
10. Spoke in the name of the Lord – 2 Chronicles 33:18; Ezekiel 3:11; James 5:10
11. Frequently spoke in parables and riddles – 2 Samuel 12:1-6; Isaiah 5:1-7; Ezekiel 17:2-10

Cultivating the Spirit of Elijah and Jehu

12. Frequently in their actions were made signs to the people – Isaiah 20:2-4; Jeremiah 19:1,10,11; 27:2,3; 43:9; 51:63; Ezekiel 4:1-13; 5:1-4; 7:23; 12:3-7; 21:6,7; 24:1-24; Hosea 1:2-9
13. Frequently left without divine communication on account of sins of the people – 1 Samuel 28:6; Lamentations 2:9; Ezekiel 7:26
14. Were required:
    a. To be bold and undaunted – Ezekiel 2:6; 3:8,9
    b. To be vigilant and faithful – Ezekiel 3:17-21
    c. To receive with attention all God's communications – Ezekiel 3:10
    d. Not to speak anything but what they received from God – Deuteronomy 18:20
    e. To declare everything that the Lord commanded – Jeremiah 26:2
15. Sometimes received divine communications and uttered predictions under great bodily and mental excitement – Jeremiah 23:9; Ezekiel 3:14,15; Daniel 7:28; 10:8; Habakkuk 3:2,16
16. Sometimes uttered their predictions in verse – Deuteronomy 32:44; Isaiah 5:1
17. Often accompanied by music while predicting – 1 Samuel 10:5; 2 Kings 3:15
18. Often committed their predictions to writing – 2 Chronicles 21:12; Jeremiah 36:2
19. Writings of read in the synagogues every Sabbath – Luke 4:17; Acts 13:15
20. Ordinary:
    a. Numerous in Israel – 1 Samuel 10:5; 1 Kings 18:4
    b. Trained up and instructed in schools – 2 Kings 2:3,5; 1 Samuel 19:20
    c. The sacred bards of the Jews – Exodus 15:20,21; 1 Samuel 10:5,10; 1 Chronicles 25:1
21. Extraordinary:
    a. Specially raised up on occasions of emergency – 1 Samuel 3:19-21; Isaiah 6:8,9; Jeremiah 1:5

      b. Often endued with miraculous power – Exodus 4:1-4; 1 Kings 17:23; 2 Kings 5:3-8
22. Frequently were married men – 2 Kings 4:1; Ezekiel 24:18
23. Often wore a coarse dress of hair-cloth – 2 Kings 1:8; Zechariah 13:4; Matthew 3:4; Revelation 11:3
24. Often led a wandering and unsettled life – 1 Kings 18:10-12; 19:3,8,15; 2 Kings 4:10
25. Simple in their manner of life – Matthew 3:4.
26. The historiographers of the Jewish nation – 1 Chronicles 29:29; 2 Chronicles 9:29
27. The interpreters of dreams – Daniel 1:17
28. Were consulted in all difficulties – 1 Samuel 9:6; 28:15; 1 Kings 14:2-4; 22:7
29. Presented with gifts by those who consulted them – 1 Samuel 9:7,8; 1 Kings 14:3
30. Sometimes thought it right to reject presents – 2 Kings 5:15,16
31. Were sent to:
    a. Reprove the wicked and exhort to repentance – 2 Kings 17:13; 2 Chronicles 24:19; Jeremiah 25:4,5
    b. Denounce the wickedness of kings – 1 Samuel 15:10,16-19; 2 Samuel 12:7-12; 1 Kings 18:18; 21:17-22
    c. Exhort to faithfulness and constancy in God's service – 2 Chronicles 15:1,2,7
    d. Predict the coming of Christ – Luke 24:44; John 1:45; Acts 3:24; 10:43
    e. Predict the downfall of nations – Isaiah 15:1; 17:1; Jeremiah chapters 47-51
32. Felt deeply on account of the calamities that they predicted – Isaiah 16:9-11; Jeremiah 9:1-7
33. Predictions of:
    a. Frequently proclaimed at the gate of the Lord's house – Jeremiah 7:2
    b. Proclaimed in the cities and streets – Jeremiah 11:6

Cultivating the Spirit of Elijah and Jehu

   c. Written on tables and set up in some public place – Habakkuk 2:2
   d. Written on rolls and read to the people – Isaiah 8:1; Jeremiah 36:2
   e. Were all fulfilled – 2 Kings 10:10; Isaiah 44:26; Acts 3:18; Revelation 10:7
34. Assisted the Jews in their great national undertakings – Ezra 5:2
35. Mentioned in Scripture:
   a. Enoch – Genesis 5:21-24; Jude 1:14
   b. Noah – Genesis 9:25-27
   c. Jacob – Genesis 49:1
   d. Aaron – Exodus 7:1
   e. Moses – Deuteronomy 18:18
   f. Miriam – Exodus 15:20
   g. Deborah – Judges 4:4
   h. Prophet sent to Israel – Judges 6:8
   i. Prophet sent to Eli – 1 Samuel 2:27
   j. Samuel – 1 Samuel 3:20
   k. David – Psalms 16:8-11; Acts 2:25,30
   l. Nathan – 2 Samuel 7:2; 12:1; 1 Kings 1:10
   m. Zadok – 2 Samuel 15:27
   n. Gad – 2 Samuel 24:11; 1 Chronicles 29:29
   o. Ahijah – 1 Kings 11:29; 12:15; 2 Chronicles 9:29
   p. Prophet of Judah – 1 Kings 13:1
   q. Iddo – 2 Chronicles 9:29; 12:15
   r. Shemaiah – 1 Kings 12:22; 2 Chronicles 12:7,15
   s. Azariah the son of Oded – 2 Chronicles 15:2,8
   t. Hanani – 2 Chronicles 16:7
   u. Jehu the son of Hanani – 1 Kings 16:1,7,12
   v. Elijah – 1 Kings 17:1
   w. Elisha – 1 Kings 19:16
   x. Micaiah the son of Imlah – 1 Kings 22:7,8
   y. Jonah – 2 Kings 14:25; Jonah 1:1; Matthew 12:39
   z. Isaiah – 2 Kings 19:2; 2 Chronicles 26:22; Isaiah 1:1
   aa. Hosea – Hosea 1:1

Defeating the Spirit of Jezebel

    bb. Amos – Amos 1:1; 7:14,15
    cc. Micah – Micah 1:1
    dd. Oded – 2 Chronicles 28:9
    ee. Nahum – Nahum 1:1
    ff. Joel – Joel 1:1; Acts 2:16
    gg. Zephaniah – Zephaniah 1:1
    hh. Huldah – 2 Kings 22:14
    ii. Jeduthun – 2 Chronicles 35:15
    jj. Jeremiah – 2 Chronicles 36:12,21; Jeremiah 1:1,2
    kk. Habakkuk – Habakkuk 1:1
    ll. Obadiah – Obadiah 1:1
    mm. Ezekiel – Ezekiel 1:3
    nn. Daniel – Daniel 12:11; Matthew 24:15
    oo. Haggai – Ezra 5:1; 6:14; Haggai 1:1
    pp. Zechariah son of Iddo – Ezra 5:1; Zechariah 1:1
    qq. Malachi – Malachi 1:1
    rr. Zacharias the father of John – Luke 1:67
    ss. Anna – Luke 2:36
    tt. Agabus – Acts 11:28; 21:10
    uu. Daughters of Philip – Acts 21:9
    vv. Paul – 1 Timothy 4:1
    ww. Peter – 2 Peter 2:1,2
    xx. John – Revelation 1:1

36. One generally attached to the king's household – 2 Samuel 24:11; 2 Chronicles 29:25; 35:15
37. The Jews:
    a. Required to hear and believe – Deuteronomy 18:15; 2 Chronicles 20:20
    b. Often tried to make them speak smooth things – 1 Kings 22:13; Isaiah 30:10; Amos 2:12
    c. Persecuted them – 2 Chronicles 36:16; Matthew 5:12
    d. Often imprisoned them – 1 Kings 22:27; Jeremiah 32:2; 37:15,16
    e. Often put them to death – 1 Kings 18:13; 19:10; Matthew 23:34-37

Cultivating the Spirit of Elijah and Jehu

    f. Often left without on account of sin – 1 Samuel 3:1; Psalms 74:9; Amos 8:11,12
38. Were mighty through faith – Hebrews 11:32-40
39. Great patience of under suffering – James 5:10
40. God avenged all injuries done to – 2 Kings 9:7; 1 Chronicles 16:21,22; Matthew 23:35-38; Luke 11:50
41. Christ predicted to exercise the office of – Deuteronomy 18:15; Acts 3:22
42. Christ exercised the office of – Matthew chapters 24 and 25; Mark 10:32-34

The following is both a scriptural and historical look at prophetic ministry with a chronological chart showing the order of the prophets:[xviii]

1. The Pre-Exilic Prophets

    Joel c. 850 B.C.
    Jonah c. 800 B.C.
    Amos c. 780-755 B.C.
    Hosea c. 760-710 B.C.
    Micah c. 740 B.C.
    Isaiah c. 740-680 B.C.
    Nahum c. 666-615 B.C.
    Zephaniah c. 630-620 B.C.
    Habakkuk c. 627-586 B.C.
    Jeremiah c. 626-580 B.C.

2. The Exilic Prophets

    Daniel c. 604-535 B.C.
    Ezekiel c. 593-570 B.C.
    Obadiah c. 585 B.C.

3. The Post-Exilic Prophets

    Haggai 520 B.C.
    Zechariah 520-518 B.C.
    Malachi c. 450-400 B.C.

The O.T. prophets were men raised up by God in times of declension and apostasy in Israel. They were primarily revivalists and patriots speaking on behalf of God to the heart and conscience of the nation.

The prophetic messages have a twofold character: (1) that which was local and for the prophet's time, and (2) that which was predictive of the divine purpose in the future. Often the prediction sprang immediately from the local circumstance (e.g. Isaiah 7:1-11 with vs. 12-14).

For prophetic ministry to be understood and received in this hour, we need God to continue to raise up prophets with integrity and ethics in the manner of their operation. Many churches have fettered their pulpits by not allowing prophetic ministry to operate in their midst. This sometimes is due to misuse and abuse by unethical prophetic ministers. Often this is also due to a breakdown in communication and relationship with the pastor.

The relationship between the prophetic minister and the pastor is perhaps the most vital of relationships. The pastor is the lifeline between the prophetic minister and the body of Christ. Thus the relationship between the pastor and the prophetic minister must be maintained continually with humility and a spirit of forgiveness. Sometimes the prophetic minister will seek to manipulate the trust that is extended to him to saints and seek financial gain or continue to make contact directly with saints to manipulate their time or involvement. This should not be! All contact with saints must be with the pastor's knowledge and permission. We must remember it is the pastor that extends the invitation to the prophet to minister to his flock, not the saint, thus the prophet must remain in good communication and relationship with the pastor at all times.

Cultivating the Spirit of Elijah and Jehu

Some misled prophetic ministers force pastors to let them receive their own offerings, thus coming up with carnal gimmicks such as, "Reserve your personal prophecy and personal prophetic ministry time for only $____." Or, "Come, shake my hand and give me $100 and receive a prophetic blessing from God!" Or they will spend inordinate amounts of time taking offerings. Their justification is a few bad experiences where a pastor maybe did not give them a very large offering. This really reveals that this prophetic minister truly does not trust God to be his provider and has the spirit of Gehazi! (See 2 Kings 5:20-27). I believe, as true proven prophets with integrity and Christian character rise up in this hour, God will confirm them with mighty signs and wonders in their ministries!

While the gift or word from God is perfect, the person ministering the gift or word is not. The pure gifts of the Spirit must flow through impure vessels of clay. A prophetic minister must never feel it is beneath him to admit a mistake. God will bless him if he remains humble and teachable in all instances of ministry. One reason the enemy resists the prophetic ministry is because the prophetic ministry deals with healing of the mind. I have witnessed many instances where a child of God was battle worn and weary in their mind when a spoken revelatory word of hope brought healing and the strength for victory.

The enemy attacks the minds of the children of God daily with torments, doubts, fears, depression, etc. The word of revelation brings healing to the mind. In the garden, the enemy attacked Eve's mind with the question, "Has God indeed said?"

Genesis 3:1, "Now the serpent was more cunning than any beast of the field which the LORD God had made. And he said to the woman, "Has God indeed said, 'You shall not eat of every tree of the garden'?" (NKJV)

The serpent honed in on the fact that Eve did not truly know what God had commanded them and, by adding a few words to the original word from God, the serpent twisted Eve's mind into an act of disobedience.

It has been expressed to me that most problems pastors have had concerning prophetic ministry were usually the result of a simple misunderstanding. Either the prophetic word was misunderstood or misinterpreted. For this reason I strongly recommend that all prophetic words be recorded for accuracy and future review. Private (non-recorded) prophecies are extremely hard to confirm and recall accurately. Even one misplaced word or misinterpreted word can affect the entire prophetic word given.

I recall a prophetic word I had spoken over a church in Texas. The word contained the phrase, "April 1997 will be the beginning of your financial miracle." This particular church and pastor had been through a season of tremendous financial difficulty and were very excited over this word. On April 15, 1997, I received a phone call from the very excited pastor because that morning he had unexpectedly received a check in the mail for several thousand dollars. After a few weeks, this same pastor called in dismay because their actual need was *several hundred thousand dollars*. He said, "Brother Arcovio, I don't understand; I thought God said we would receive our financial miracle in April of 1997." I replied, "Brother, do you have the *exact wording* of that prophetic word?" He replied, "Yes, I have the tape right now." I then instructed him to repeat the word to me. It was then that he realized that the word actually stated *"the beginning . . ."* Truly this unexpected check was the "little cloud, like a man's hand."

Within six months this church had all the finances they needed.

The relationship between the prophetic minister and the believer is perhaps the most fragile part of the relationship. This is particularly true in situations where the believer is a young Christian or has not received the proper teaching concerning prophecy and the true nature of the prophetic ministry. The following Scripture is a good prophetic principle to live by.

Psalm 131:1,2, *"¹LORD, my heart is not haughty, Nor my eyes lofty. Neither do I concern myself with great matters, Nor with things too profound for me. ²Surely I have calmed and quieted my soul, Like a weaned child with his mother; Like a weaned child is my soul within me."* (NKJV)

The prophet must be more like a child in his spirit than anything. He must be easily entreated, able to receive correction and rebuke and walk in humility and simplicity with respect to the gift God has given him. Many prophetic ministers have hindered their ability to be received with attitudes of pride, independence, self-will, and un-teachableness. They exude the air that their gift makes them accountable to no one, and that they are greater than all ministries. This results in their eventual demise and in bringing dishonor to the Kingdom of God.

The first thing God gave the prophet Samuel, before He ever began revealing His secrets to him, was favor with Himself and men.

1 Samuel 2:26, "And the child Samuel grew on, and was in favour both with the LORD, and also with men." [xix]

The prophet who enters the "limelight" too soon will be tempted to seek the favor of men over God. He will be molded by the pulpits he speaks in instead of being molded by the hand of God. Many become "for hire."

It does not matter how anointed our lives are, how gifted our ministry, or how accurate the revelatory word operates within us, to be effective, men must have love, faith, respect, and trust in us. The early stages of our ministry will mainly be involved with the Lord establishing His favor upon our lives in response to our willingness to fast and pray with a focused, humble, broken, and contrite spirit. It is when we respond to the relationships of life with a spirit of humility and brokenness (total dependence upon God) that we are received by men and receive more from God. As God establishes favor in our ministries, then He will begin to increase the Oikios (circle of influence) of authority and influence of our ministry. We can observe this in continuing to look at the life of the prophet Samuel:

1 Samuel 3:19-21, "[19]So Samuel grew, and the LORD was with him and let none of his words fall to the ground. [20]And all Israel from Dan to Beersheba knew that Samuel *had been* established as a prophet of the LORD. [21]Then the LORD appeared again in Shiloh. For the LORD revealed Himself to Samuel in Shiloh by the word of the LORD." (NKJV)

The place where prophetic and revelatory word is the most useful and operative is in the prophet's personal intimacy and walk with God. The pure operation of the gifts is found in talking to Jesus and Him talking intimately with us. This is where we can fine tune, fine point, and truly be led by the Holy Ghost.

God will first reveal Himself to us through the intimacy of His Word before He begins to reveal His secrets concerning others or other situations. Knowing the voice of God for oneself in correction, instruction, and guidance is of utmost importance! In the past five books that God has given to me, the emphasis of intimacy with Jesus and knowing His voice has been reiterated. Even though repetition is the greatest teacher, I know I must be sounding like a broken record by now. Nevertheless, I must again emphasize the absolute importance that *a prophetic minister knows the voice of God for his own life first!* Many young ministers mistakenly think they can "learn" to prophesy by reading books written by prophetic ministers, listening to tape series, or even attending prophetic seminars. While all these ministry resource materials have their place, they can never replace a man of God's need for an intimate walk with God.

I have even read advertisements in popular denominational magazines that (for a healthy fee) "guarantee" a prophetic word or a closed session where the "prophet's" gift will be imparted by the simple laying on of a hand.

This reminds me of a service where a young man came forward and asked for a minister to lay hands on him and pray for him. This misguided young man looked up at the minister and said, "Lay your hands on me and bestow your gifts on me." The minister paused and then laid his hands upon him and began to pray, "Oh, Lord, let this young man be stripped of everything that he owns down to the clothes on his back. Let him lose his family and honor. Let this young man suffer much persecution and misunderstanding at the hands of friends while trying to sincerely serve you. Let him sleep many months in a sleeping bag, in ten-degree temperature in the back of a camper truck while fasting and praying for doors to open for his ministry. Let him serve and give faithfully for many years while seemingly nothing is every given in return. Let his body suffer tremendously in health from the many nights of all-night prayer and weeks of extended fasting." While the minister was praying, the young man began to pull away looking confused. He was looking for a "quick fix" and a "cheap anointing."

This is why Paul's heart echoed the cry in Philippians 3:8-10:

"8Yet indeed I also count all things loss for the excellence of the knowledge of Christ Jesus my Lord, for whom I have suffered the loss of all things, and count them as rubbish, that I may gain Christ 9and be found in Him, not having my own righteousness, which *is* from the law, but that which *is* through faith in Christ, the righteousness which is from God by faith; 10that I may know Him and the power of His resurrection, and the fellowship of His sufferings, being conformed to His death," (NKJV)

It was this type of intimacy with God that caused Enoch to be translated into the presence of God, Abraham to sacrifice Isaac and be called the friend of God, Moses to cry, "Show my thy Glory," and Mary to sit at the feet of Jesus and move the Lord to say;

Luke 10:42, "But one thing is needed, and Mary has chosen that good part, which will not be taken away from her." (NKJV)

When we choose to commit our lives foremost to intimacy with Jesus, no matter what trials or hardships come our way, trials by family, friend, or foe, our relationship with Jesus will take us through.

For this reason Jesus said in John 15:15:

"No longer do I call you servants, for a servant does not know what his master is doing; but I have called you friends, for all things that I heard from My Father I have made known to you."[xx]

There is a great difference in being a servant of God and entering into that special relationship of a friend. A servant accomplishes his master's will with relatively no intimate relationship with him. A friend comes to know not just the intent and purposes of the master and to accomplish them as though the master was there present, but he also comes to know the person of the master and enter into a relationship of friendship with him. This is the same as the difference between a wife and a maid. A maid will enter the bedroom to clean and fix-up, but when the wife enters the bedroom it is often for an entirely different intimate relationship. Often the fruit of the womb is produced from this intimacy. Thus the church, as the bride of Christ, receives the purpose and intent of God into its "spiritual womb" and eventually brings forth the intended purpose of God.

There is no such thing as a "cheap anointing." There is a great price to be paid to be a true prophet of God who is established with favor in the eyes of God and man, and whose spoken revelatory words never fall to the ground void. True anointing oil from God comes with a high price tag. In Exodus 30:23-25 and 31-38 there are eight spices mentioned:

"23Take thou also unto thee principal spices, of pure myrrh five hundred *shekels*, and of sweet cinnamon half so much, *even* two hundred and fifty *shekels*, and of sweet calamus two hundred and fifty shekels, 24And of cassia five hundred *shekels*, after the shekel of the sanctuary, and of oil olive an hin: 25And thou shalt make it an oil of holy ointment, an ointment compound after the art of the apothecary {g apothecary or perfumer}: it shall be an holy anointing oil.

"31And thou shalt speak unto the children of Israel, saying, This shall be an holy anointing oil unto me throughout your generations. 32Upon man's flesh shall it not be poured, neither shall ye make *any other* like it, after the composition of it: it *is* holy, *and* it shall be holy unto you. ³³Whosoever compoundeth *any* like it, or whosoever putteth *any* of it upon a stranger, shall even be cut off from his people.

³⁴And the LORD said unto Moses, Take unto thee sweet spices, stacte, and onycha, and galbanum; *these* sweet spices with pure frankincense: of each shall there be a like *weight:* ³⁵And thou shalt make it a perfume, a confection after the art of the apothecary, tempered {h tempered . . .: Heb. salted} together, pure and holy: ³⁶And thou shalt beat *some* of it very small, and put of it before the testimony in the tabernacle of the congregation, where I will meet with thee: it shall be unto you most holy. ³⁷And *as for* the perfume which thou shalt make, ye shall not make to yourselves according to the composition thereof: it shall be unto thee holy for the LORD. ³⁸Whosoever shall make like unto that, to smell thereto, shall even be cut off from his people."[xxi]

This holy anointing oil was compounded only after much labor and effort. The spices were gathered from all over the world. Here is an example of where some of these spices came from:

Verse 23, [Principal spices] i.e. the best spices. [Pure myrrh] is a gum that comes from the stem of a low, thorny, ragged tree that grows in Arabia Felix and Eastern Africa called by botanists Balsamodendron myrrha. The word here rendered 'pure' is literally "freely flowing," an epithet that is explained by the fact that the best myrrh is said to exude spontaneously from the bark, while that of inferior quality oozes out in greater quantity from incisions made in the bark.

[Five hundred shekels] was probably rather more than 15¼ pounds (see Exodus 38:24).

[Cinnamon] is obtained from a tree allied to the laurel that grows in Ceylon (Sri Lanka) and other islands of the Indian Ocean known in botany as the Cinnamomum zeylanicum. It is the inner rind of the tree dried in the sun. It was imported from India in very early times by the people of Ophir and brought with other spices from the south part of Arabia by the trading caravans that visited Egypt and Syria. The mention of these spices in Exodus may be taken as the earliest notice we have connected with commerce with the remote East.

[Two hundred and fifty shekels] about 7 pounds, 14 ounces.

[Sweet calamus] This fragrant cane (or rush) was probably what is now known in India as the Lemon Grass.

Verse 24, [Cassia] is the inner bark of an Indian tree (Cinnamomum cassia), which differs from that which produces cinnamon in the shape of its leaves and some other particulars. It was probably in ancient times, as it is at present, by far less costly than cinnamon, and it may have been on this account that it was used in double quantity.

[An hin] Probably about six pints (see Leviticus 19:36).

Verse 25, [An oil of holy ointment] Rather, a holy anointing oil.

[After the art of the apothecary] According to Jewish tradition, the essences of the spices were first extracted and then mixed with the oil. The preparation of the anointing oil, as well as of the incense, was entrusted to Bezaleel (Exodus 37:29), and the care of preserving it to Eleazar the son of Aaron (Numbers 4:16).

In a later age, it was prepared by the sons of the priests (1 Chronicles 9:30).

Verse 32, [Upon man's flesh] i.e. on the persons of those who were not priests who might employ it for such anointing as was usual on festive occasions (see Psalms 104:15; Proverbs 27:9; Matthew 6:17, etc.).

Verse 33, [A stranger] see Exodus 29:33. [Cut off from his people] see Exodus 31:14.

(Exodus 37:29) The incense, like the anointing oil, consisted of four aromatic ingredients.

[Stacte] supposed to be either the gum of the Storax tree (Styrax officinale) found in Syria and the neighboring countries, or the gum known as Benzoin, or Gum Benjamin, which is an important ingredient in the incense now used in churches and mosques and is the product of another storax tree (Styrax benzoin) that grows in Java and Sumatra.

[Onycha], a perfume perhaps made from the cap of the strombus, or wing-shell, which abounds in the Red Sea.

[Galbanum], a gum of a yellowish brown color, in the form of either grains or masses. It is imported from India, Persia, and Africa, but the plant from which it comes is not yet certainly known.

[Pure frankincense] This was the most important of the aromatic gums. Like myrrh, it was regarded by itself as a precious perfume (Song of Solomon 3:6; Matthew 2:11), and it was used unmixed with other substances in some of the rites of the law. The tree from which it is obtained is not found in Arabia. It was most likely imported from India by the Sabaeans like Cinnamon, Cassia, and Calamus (see Exodus 30:23). The tree is now known as the Boswellia serrata, or B. thurifera, and grows abundantly in the highlands of India. The frankincense of commerce is a different substance and is the resin of the spruce and of some other kinds of fir.[xxii]

When we allow God to use the anvil and hammer of life to break and mold us, then God can entrust us with the true, pure anointing from on high to flow through us to a hurting generation. We develop and discover this anointing in the daily discovery of the "still small voice."

The prophet Elijah discovered that the Lord often speaks in the "still small voice." In 1 Kings 19, Elijah had gone out into the wilderness to flee the wrath of Queen Jezebel. He was at a very low point in his life no doubt suffering from a low self-image. His trust and faith in God had "bottomed out." He had what I call a "cave mentality" feeling that he was all alone, the only one suffering, the only one walking this path of loneliness. Elijah was having, if you will, a "pity party." The only problem with having a "pity party" is that nobody else shows up. Fortunately for Elijah, the Lord decided to show up at his pity party. Let's look at the scriptural account of the meeting:

1 Kings 19:9-13, "⁹And there he went into a cave, and spent the night in that place; and behold, the word of the LORD *came* to him, and He said to him, "What are you doing here, Elijah?" ¹⁰So he said, "I have been very zealous for the LORD God of hosts; for the children of Israel have forsaken Your covenant, torn down Your altars, and killed Your prophets with the sword. I alone am left; and they seek to take my life.

"¹¹Then He said, "Go out, and stand on the mountain before the LORD." And behold, the LORD passed by, and a great and strong wind tore into the mountains and broke the rocks in pieces before the LORD, *but* the LORD *was* not in the wind; and after the wind an earthquake, *but* the LORD *was* not in the earthquake; ¹²and after the earthquake a fire, *but* the Lord *was* not in the fire; and after the fire a still small voice. ¹³So it was, when Elijah heard *it*, that he wrapped his face in his mantle and went out and stood in the entrance of the cave. Suddenly a voice *came* to him, and said, "What are you doing here, Elijah?" (NKJV)

The word 'still' in verse 12 is translated from the Hebrew word d'emamah (dem-aw-maw), which means silence, whisper, calm.[xxiii]

Elijah did not discover the Word of the Lord in the wind (what he could hear with his human ears), or in the earthquake (what he could feel in his human emotions), or in the fire (what he could see with his human eyes). He found the Word of the Lord in the still small voice (time of quite awe and reverent fear). In like manner, when we seek to discover the still, small voice of God, it will not be discerned by our natural hearing, eyesight, or our human emotions. It will be discovered within our human spirit as we quiet ourselves and become "still" before him. Obviously we cannot listen and talk simultaneously. It must be one or the other.

What the Lord was trying to impress upon Elijah was that, even though He could use Elijah to call down fire from heaven or to shake the foundations of kingdoms, when all the flash and grandeur of these supernatural operations were past, it was the intimacy of walking with His Creator and knowing His still, small voice that would keep him through the lonely nights of discouragement and oppression from the enemy. We must know Him!

As New Testament believers, we can learn from this account not to always be looking for a mighty manifestation of God's power to confirm His presence in our daily lives. We should be seeking to be sensitive to

His presence in that still, small voice even when we can't seem to feel, see, or hear His workings. As the saying goes, "When you can see His hand, trust His heart." We can also learn not to allow any emotion or circumstance to cause us to waver from doing what God has spoken to us to do.

The Bible Knowledge Commentary makes the following comment on 2 Kings 19:11-14:

> Standing on the mountainside outside his cave, Elijah witnessed what Moses had seen in those mountains centuries before (Exodus 19:16-18), and what he himself had seen on Mount Carmel only a few days earlier (1 Kings 18:38,45), namely, a spectacular demonstration of the power of God, this time in wind, an earthquake, and fire. But on this occasion the Lord was not in any of these, that is, they were not His instruments of self-revelation.
>
> Evidently, some time later when Elijah was back in his cave (19:13), he heard the sound of a gentle whisper. Recognizing this as a revelation of God, he pulled his cloak over part of his face, walked out to the mouth of the cave, and stood there waiting for God to act. God asked the same question He asked earlier: "What are you doing here, Elijah?" The prophet's response was identical to his first reply suggesting that, even though he may have understood the point of God's display of natural forces for his benefit, he still felt the same way about himself.
>
> The message God seems to have intended for Elijah is that, whereas He had revealed Himself in spectacular demonstrations of His power in the past at Kerith, Zarephath, and Carmel, He would now use Elijah in gentler, less dramatic ways. These ways God proceeded to explain to His servant (verses 15-18). God

Defeating the Spirit of Jezebel

would deal with Elijah's personal feelings about himself later in a gentle way too.[xxiv]

I believe this also expresses the manner in which God would speak through modern day prophets today. Whereas the Old Testament prophets experienced a lot of natural phenomenon (i.e. fire, wind, visible hands writing on walls) in connection with the receiving of the Word of God, New Testament prophets seem to receive a word from God mainly through impressions and the still, small voice.

This also makes the New Testament prophets more vulnerable to "missing" the voice of God or "misinterpreting" a true word from God (possibly one reason why we don't stone a prophet who "misses" in this day).

As I said before, I will emphasize again, all ministry must flow from our relationship with God. Our daily intimacy with God can be compared to natural breathing in life. This exchange of spiritual relationship and intimacy is the breath of God. All prophetic ministries should flow from the breath of God.

It is recorded in Genesis 2:7:

"And the LORD God formed man of the dust of the ground, and breathed into his nostrils the breath of life; and man became a living soul."

A prophetic word is the Breath of Life from God! Church, it is time to stop trying to hold your breath.

We have a mechanism in us that makes us breathe. You can't commit suicide by not breathing; you must breathe. Your body makes you breathe.

You can go a few days without water, and a little longer than a month without food, but you cannot live a moment without breath. If you held your breath, in a few moments there would be a burning in your chest. Your face would turn red, your body would scream – BREATHE!!!

Then you would breathe in great gasps, drinking in the air. Respiration is what they call it in medical books. You inhale oxygen and you exhale carbon dioxide. While breathing in, air goes into your lungs, and oxygen is transferred into your blood. While breathing out, the result of respiration, the by-product, carbon dioxide, is exhaled and removed from your body.

Until God breathed on Adam, Adam was only a shell of a man, but when God breathed, Adam was a living man. Life comes from God, and that life is His breath.

Look at Ezekiel in chapter 37. God takes him to a valley of dry bones scattered here and there with no order of any kind, and God tells him to prophesy to this valley of dry bones.

With his prophesying there is a whole lot of shaking going on. The bones get together, and then muscles and skin cover the bones. Bones that were dry and disjoined are no longer disjoined, but they are still not alive. There is order, but order without life.

Then the prophet prophesies to the wind, and the wind blows. The valley of dead soldiers becomes a living, breathing, standing army of great number. The only thing that can take your valley of dead, dry bones and turn it into something of any goodness is God.

The prophet spoke in the valley. He was in the midst of a valley. He was in the middle of a bad memory. Here all around him were the remnants of a great destruction. Talk about skeletons in a closet, he had a valley full of skeletons.

Here he was in a valley of bad memories, in a valley of dead, dry bones. God instructed the prophet to prophesy to them. Ezekiel obeys and watches as the "foot bone connects to the ankle bone, and the ankle bone connects to the leg bone, the . . ."; you get the picture, and then muscles and flesh cover the army.

We must have the wind of the Spirit blowing in our midst if the army is going to stand up, live, and minister.

One thing they teach all expecting mothers is how to breathe. Their concern is that the mother might get so preoccupied with the birth that she will forget to breathe. Breathing is vitally important because she is breathing for two.

The church is pregnant with child. The church is burdened. We must not get so preoccupied with our burden that we forget to breathe in daily intimacy with God. We are breathing for more than two. We are breathing for the world.

Now back to the five-fold ministry.

Timothy the Pastor (the ring finger of God)

As I mentioned before, the pastor can be compared to the index finger that is commonly recognized as the "ring finger." This is the symbol of the union of marriage. The pastor or shepherd's burden is to prepare the bride (church) to be joined with the bridegroom (Jesus) at His coming.

It is commonly understood that Timothy was the pastor of the church in Ephesus.

1 Timothy 1:3, "As I urged you when I went into Macedonia — remain in *Ephesus* that you may charge some that they teach no other doctrine," (NKJV)

Timothy also went with Paul on the journey to Jerusalem with the collection (Acts 20:4,5) and is next heard of when Paul, then a prisoner, wrote Colossians, Philemon, and Philippians. In the latter epistle, Timothy is warmly commended, and Paul intends to soon send him to them in order to ascertain their welfare. When the apostle was released from his imprisonment and engaged in further activity in the E{E East, eastern; Elohist}, as the Pastoral Epistles indicate, it would seem that Paul left Timothy at Ephesus (1 Timothy 1:3) and commissioned him to deal with false teachers and supervise public worship and the appointment of church officials.[xxv]

We can observe in 2 Timothy 4:5 that, even though Timothy's primary ministry was that of a pastor, he also was involved in the ministry of the evangelist.

"But you be watchful in all things, endure afflictions, do the work of an evangelist, fulfill your ministry."

The pastor is commonly understood to be the shepherd or overseer.

Acts 20:28, "Therefore take heed to yourselves and to all the flock, among which the Holy Spirit has made you overseers, to shepherd the church of God which He purchased with His own blood." (NKJV)

The following are some tasks the natural shepherd has which can also be compared to the spiritual shepherd or pastor:
- to watch for enemies trying to attack the sheep
- to defend the sheep from attackers
- to heal the wounded and sick sheep
- to find and save lost or trapped sheep
- to love them, sharing their lives and so earning their trust

During World War II, a shepherd pilot was one who guided another pilot whose plane was partially disabled back to the base or carrier by flying alongside him to maintain visual contact. It is also the spiritual duty of New Testament shepherds to assist in helping wounded people find their way back to the sheepfold.

Phillip the Evangelist (the middle finger of God)

The evangelist can be likened unto the middle finger, the longest of all the fingers on the hand. The evangelist is the most adept at reaching into the world and pulling out the harvest of souls.

Acts 21:8, "On the next day we who were Paul's companions departed and came to Caesarea, and entered the house of Philip the evangelist, who was one of the seven, and stayed with him." (NKJV)

We can observe this ministry of evangelism during one of the revivals recorded in Acts 8:5-16:

"5Then Philip went down to the city of Samaria and preached Christ to them. 6And the multitudes with one accord heeded the things spoken by Philip, hearing and seeing the miracles which he did. 7For unclean spirits, crying with a loud voice, came out of many who were possessed; and many who were paralyzed and lame were healed. 8And there was great joy in that city. 9But there was a certain man called Simon, who previously practiced sorcery in the city and astonished the people of Samaria, claiming that he was someone great, 10to whom they all gave heed, from the least to the greatest, saying, "This man is the great power of God." 11And they heeded him because he had astonished them with his sorceries for a long time. 12But when they believed Philip as he preached the things concerning the kingdom of God and the name of Jesus Christ, both men and women were baptized. 13Then Simon himself also believed; and when he was baptized he continued with Philip, and was amazed, seeing the miracles and signs which were done.

¹⁴Now when the apostles who were at Jerusalem heard that Samaria had received the word of God, they sent Peter and John to them, ¹⁵who, when they had come down, prayed for them that they might receive the Holy Spirit. ¹⁶For as yet He had fallen upon none of them. They had only been baptized in the name of the Lord Jesus."

Many Teachers (the pinky of God)

Acts 13:1, "Now in the church that was at Antioch there were certain prophets and teachers: Barnabas, Simeon who was called Niger, Lucius of Cyrene, Manaen who had been brought up with Herod the tetrarch, and Saul." (NKJV)

The pinky appears to be the smallest of the fingers of the hand, thus the least important, but it is the pinky that gives the hand the strength in grip. Without the pinky, the hand would have no strength. In the same manner, the "pinky toe" on our foot is what gives us the ability to keep our balance. The ministry of the teacher is often the least recognized but, without the "grounding" ministry of the teacher, the church would have no spiritual strength or balance. The teacher is anointed with a special ability that God gives to certain members of the Body of Christ to communicate information relevant to the health and ministry of the Body and its members in such a way that others will learn and be rooted and grounded in apostolic truths. An anointed apostolic teacher has the ability to communicate in simplicity spiritual truths that may otherwise be difficult to understand. Therefore, the ministry of the teacher is a vital component in establishing the full "length, breadth, height, and width" of the true apostolic church.

Here in this passage the Scriptures point out that the ministry of prophets and teachers was alive and well many years after the establishing of the First Church. Apostolic revival comes in the midst of apostolic order. Tradition is probably one of the greatest enemies to the church in understanding and receiving the five-fold ministry.

Mark 7:13, "Making the word of God of none effect through your tradition, which ye have delivered: and many such like things do ye."

Because of tradition, many would rather call someone "reverend," "doctor," "superintendent," or "bishop." But they consider using "apostle" or "prophet" to be extreme and may even try to ignore, avoid, or attack those operating in these biblical offices. The purpose for a title is to identify a ministry's function. An office is a position of authority, duty, or trust given to a person. It has never been the will of God for an office to be vacant. Most churches would never think of going very long without a pastor but will try to fill that position as soon as possible, yet some will try to deny or ignore other offices of the five-fold ministry. Paul referred to his title "apostle" as being an office.

Romans 11:13, "For I speak to you Gentiles, inasmuch as I am the apostle of the Gentiles, I magnify mine office:"

Those who dare to proclaim Apostolic Order with boldness will be labeled as "controversial" and "troublemakers." But if that's what it takes to be Apostolic, then we will endure those labels in Jesus Name!

Endnotes:

---

[i] New International Version
[ii] Ibid
[iii] Ibid
[iv] Biblesoft's New Exhaustive Strong's Numbers and Concordance with Expanded Greek-Hebrew Dictionary. Copyright (c) 1994, Biblesoft and International Bible Translators, Inc.
[v] Ibid
[vi] Ibid
[vii] Ibid
[viii] Ibid
[ix] Ibid
[x] Ibid
[xi] John Eckhardt, Moving in the Apostolic (Gospel Light Publications, Ventura, California) 1999.
[xii] Walvoord, John F., and Zuck, Roy B., The Bible Knowledge Commentary, (Wheaton, Illinois: Scripture Press Publications, Inc.) 1983, 1985.
[xiii] NKJV
[xiv] Biblesoft's New Exhaustive Strong's Numbers and Concordance with Expanded Greek-Hebrew Dictionary. Copyright (c) 1994, Biblesoft and International Bible Translators, Inc.
[xv] Ibid
[xvi] John Eckhardt, Moving in the Apostolic (Gospel Light Publications, Ventura, California, 1999)
[xvii] Biblesoft's New Exhaustive Strong's Numbers and Concordance with Expanded Greek-Hebrew Dictionary. Copyright (c) 1994, Biblesoft and International Bible Translators, Inc.
[xviii] New Scofield Reference Edition Bible, Oxford University Press, 1967 Edition, on page 711 and 712 an article.
[xix] The New King James Version.
[xx] Ibid
[xxi] Ibid
[xxii] from Barnes' Notes, Electronic Database. Copyright (c) 1997 by Biblesoft
[xxiii] *Enhanced Strong's Lexicon*, (Oak Harbor, WA: Logos Research Systems, Inc.) 1995.
[xxiv] Walvoord, John F., and Zuck, Roy B., *The Bible Knowledge Commentary*, (Wheaton, Illinois: Scripture Press Publications, Inc.) 1983, 1985.
[xxv] The New Bible Dictionary, (Wheaton, Illinois: Tyndale House Publishers, Inc.) 1962.

3
Defeating the Spirit of Jezebel

The following are several principles that help to defeat Jezebel.

1. Repentance
2. Humility
3. Intercession
4. Submission to authority
5. Prophetic ministry

Repentance:

Jezebel absolutely despises repentance. Jezebel will not repent due to her pride. This is why confronting Jezebel always escalates into an all-out attack to destroy the person who is confronting. Jezebel would rather try to intimidate, discredit, and destroy the spiritual authority exposing her deeds. God promised us mercy if we will repent.

Isaiah 1:18-20, "¹⁸Come now, and let us reason together, saith the LORD: though your sins be as scarlet, they shall be as white as snow; though they be red like crimson, they shall be as wool. ¹⁹If ye be willing and obedient, ye shall eat the good of the land: [20]But if ye refuse and rebel, ye shall be devoured with the sword: for the mouth of the LORD hath spoken it."

Micah 7:18,19, "[18]Who *is* a God like unto thee, that pardoneth iniquity, and passeth by the transgression of the remnant of his heritage? he retaineth not his anger for ever, because he delighteth *in* mercy. [19]He will turn again, he will have compassion upon us; he will subdue our iniquities; and thou wilt cast all their sins into the depths of the sea."

Proverbs 28:13,14, "[13]He that covereth his sins shall not prosper: but whoso confesseth and forsaketh *them* shall have mercy. [14]Happy is the man that feareth alway: but he that hardeneth his heart shall fall into mischief."

Psalms 51:7,9-13,16,17, "[7]Purge me with hyssop, and I shall be clean: wash me, and I shall be whiter than snow. [9]Hide thy face from my sins, and blot out all mine iniquities. [10]Create in me a clean heart, O God; and renew a right spirit within me. [11]Cast me not away from thy presence; and take not thy holy spirit from me. [12]Restore unto me the joy of thy salvation; and uphold me *with thy* free spirit. [13]*Then* will I teach transgressors thy ways; and sinners shall be converted unto thee. [16]For thou desirest not sacrifice; else would I give *it:* thou delightest not in burnt offering. [17]The sacrifices of God *are* a broken spirit: a broken and a contrite heart, O God, thou wilt not despise."

1 John 1:9, "If we confess our sins, he is faithful and just to forgive us *our* sins, and to cleanse us from all unrighteousness."

In spite of these scriptural promises and many more, Jezebel refuses to repent. Jesus spoke of her unrepentant attitude in Revelation 2:21:

"And I gave her space to repent of her fornication; *and she repented not."* (Emphasis added)

Jezebel will not bow its knee. Jezebel may cry some tears, but tears, my friend, are not repentance. Repentance is making the change; making the decision to make the "about-face" and walk in a way that is contrary to what that spirit is trying to make you do. If you're walking in immorality, walk in purity. That's repentance. Jezebel hates repentance.

Repentance is the true path to deliverance. Repentance is the one weapon that destroys the spirit of Jezebel. The spirit of Jezebel hates repentance because repentance eradicates its spirit. If you are being influenced by Jezebel, begin with repentance and you will be on the path to deliverance! I like to find the things the devil hates and do those things.

Prophets are also something Jezebel despises because prophets have the power to expose and bring repentance.

Humility:

Jezebel hates humility. Jezebel scorns and mocks humility. Jezebel will try to dominate and "run-over" the leader that exudes the spirit of humility. In a marriage, when one of the spouses is bound by the spirit of Jezebel, and the other spouse tries to show humility, the bound one will ridicule the other and scoff at the humble spirit as a weakness and will try to manipulate the partner because of their humility.

God honors and rewards the spirit of humility in a leader.

2 Chronicles 7:14, "If my people, which are called by my name, shall humble themselves, and pray, and

seek my face, and turn from their wicked ways; then will I hear from heaven, and will forgive their sin, and will heal their land."

When a leader chooses to respond with humility to the vicious attacks of Jezebel, then God will stand for him and fight his battle, destroying the works of Jezebel.

1 Peter 5:5,6, "⁵Likewise, ye younger, submit yourselves unto the elder. Yea, all *of you* be subject one to another, and be clothed with humility: for God resisteth the proud, and giveth grace to the humble. ⁶Humble yourselves therefore under the mighty hand of God, that he may exalt you in due time:"

The phrase "resisteth the proud" comes from the Greek word NT:498 antitassomai (an-tee-tas'-som-ahee); from NT:473 and the middle voice of NT:5021; to range oneself against, i.e. oppose: KJV – oppose themselves, resist.[i]

If we choose to respond to situations of life with an attitude of pride, then the devil does not have to resist us for God opposes us! Nothing we attempt can be successful if God opposes us!

When a leader chooses to be humble in the midst of Jezebel's attacks, he must understand that the timetable of God's dealing with Jezebel may not be the same as his timetable.

Often you will experience incredible pain and heartache while the ungodly person affected by Jezebel will seemingly go a long period of time without God dealing with them. Remember, the judgment wheels of God may grind slowly, but they do grind finely. God is thorough and complete when He decides it is time to judge a thing. Elijah never saw Jezebel dealt with in his lifetime. Often a congregation influenced by Jezebel will be the hammer in the hand of God to develop His character and purpose in a pastor's life. My five-year pastoring in St. Joseph has been truly a "fiery furnace" in which God is instilling His purpose and purifying His vessel. Many who purposefully do things to bring you pain do not understand they are simply hammers in God's hand to bring about His purpose. Paul referred to this in Philippians 1:16:

"The one preach Christ of contention, not sincerely, supposing to add affliction to my bonds:"

Oh, the grace of God to embrace the hammers in His divine hand!

1 Kings 19:1-8, "¹And Ahab told Jezebel all that Elijah had done, and withal how he had slain all the prophets with the sword. ²Then Jezebel sent a messenger unto Elijah, saying, So let the gods do *to me,* and more also, if I make not thy life as the life of one of them by to morrow about this time. ³And when he saw *that,* he arose, and went for his life, and came to Beersheba, which *belongeth* to Judah, and left his servant there. ⁴But he himself went a day's journey into the wilderness, and came and sat down under a juniper tree: and he requested for himself that he might die; and said, It is enough; now, O LORD, take away my life; for I *am* not better than my fathers. ⁵And as he lay and slept under a juniper tree, behold, then an angel touched him, and said unto him, Arise *and* eat. ⁶And he looked, and, behold, there was a cake baken on the coals, and a cruse of water at his head. And he did eat and drink, and laid him down again. ⁷And the angel of the LORD came again the second time, and touched him, and said, Arise *and* eat; because the journey *is* too great for thee. ⁸And he arose, and did eat and drink,

and went in the strength of that meat forty days and forty nights unto Horeb the mount of God."

The hammer is a useful tool. The nail, if it had feeling and intelligence, could present another side of the story, for the nail knows the hammer only as an opponent, a brutal merciless enemy that lives to pound it into submission, to beat it down out of sight, and to clench it into place. That is the nail's view of the hammer, and it is an accurate view except for one thing. The nail forgets that both it and the hammer are servants of the same Master.

Let the nail remember that the hammer is held by the Master and all resentment toward it will disappear. The Master carpenter decides whose head shall be beaten next and what hammer shall be used in the beating. That is the sovereign right of the Master carpenter. When the nail has surrendered to the will of the workman, and has gotten a glimpse of His divine plans for its future, it will yield to the hammer without complaint.[ii]

Job 19:14-21, "¹⁴My kinsfolk have failed, and my familiar friends have forgotten me. ¹⁵They that dwell in mine house, and my maids, count me for a stranger: I am an alien in their sight. ¹⁶I called my servant, and he gave *me* no answer; I intreated him with my mouth. ¹⁷My breath is strange to my wife, though I intreated for the children's *sake* of mine own body. ¹⁸Yea, young children despised me; I arose, and they spake against me. ¹⁹All my inward friends abhorred me: and they whom I loved are turned against me. ²⁰My bone cleaveth to my skin and to my flesh, and I am escaped with the skin of my teeth. ²¹Have pity upon me, have pity upon me, O ye my friends; for the hand of God hath touched me."

Job and Elijah were sincere, dedicated servants of the Lord. Yet, when they went through a crisis in their lives, they each fell into an ocean of self-pity.

Job complained, "My breath disgusts my wife, and my relatives and closest friends have forgotten me. I'm skin and bones – just barely alive. Have pity on me everyone. Have pity on me, for God has turned against me." Likewise, Elijah moaned, "I've had enough, LORD. Just let me die! I'm no better than my ancestors (shame)."

Webster's dictionary says that self-pity is a *sympathetic, self-indulgent lingering on one's sorrows or misfortunes, often tied to the belief that one is a victim of circumstance or ill treatment.*[iii] Self-pity helps us feel better, but it provides only temporary relief. In a way, it's like morphine because it deadens our pain for a while but, before long, the pain returns.

The bad thing is that self-pity is counter-productive. Instead of promoting healing, it leads to an ongoing cycle of anger, bitterness, and depression. In fact, self-pity is a stepping-stone to such harmful emotions as anxiety, envy, depression, despair, unforgiveness, and bitterness beside such harmful responses as sulking and brooding. Self-pity is the stuff from which suicide, murder, and other serious sins are made. It's clearly self-destructive, but it's deceptive because our flesh somehow enjoys it.

In time, people who yield to self-pity gradually become angry with God for allowing them to be hurt or poorly treated (rebellion). They think, "How could God let this happen to me when I'm trying so hard to please Him?" Perhaps Elijah felt this way when he said, "God, I've always been very zealous for you. But, your people have turned against you and killed all your prophets. I'm the only one who's left, and now they're trying to kill me, too." In a way, he seems to be implying, "Aren't you going to help me, Lord?"

The divine file of God is also a painful instrument biting and eating away at the soft edges until it has shaped the metal of the spirit of man to His will. Yet the file serves another Master, as the metal also does. It is the Master and not the file that decides how much shall be eaten away, what shape the metal shall take, and how long the painful filing shall continue. Let the metal accept the will of the Master and it will not try to dictate when and how it shall be filed.

Philippians 4:13, "I can do all things through Christ which strengtheneth me."

Elijah was bold as a lion when his thoughts were centered on God. In 1 Kings 18 he called fire down from heaven, led the slaughter of 850 false prophets, and broke a three-year drought when he prayed for rain. Why, then, did he run for his life when Queen Jezebel threatened him? Surely the people would have followed him in a revolt against her!

Perhaps Jezebel's reputation got to Elijah coupled with the extreme pressure of all he'd just gone through. Whatever the case, he took his eyes off the Lord and ran for his life. Could it be that Elijah's prophetic ministry was taken away and given to Elisha because he became paralyzed with self-pity?

Self-pity is dangerous because it causes us to think irrationally. Elijah thought he was no better than his ancestors, which is a revelation of the damaging work of shame in his life. But the truth of the matter is that God used him in a mighty way! Likewise, Job felt God had become his enemy when just the opposite was true. He only experienced trouble because the Lord was using his faithfulness to rebuke Satan.

The solution to self-pity is to put the matter into God's hands, choose humility and submission, and leave it there. The Bible says that we'll have trouble in the world so give up the notion that Christians shouldn't have problems.

John 16:33, "I have told you these things, so that in me you may have peace. In this world you will have trouble. But take heart! I have overcome the world." (NIV)

1 Peter 4:12,13, "[12]Beloved, think it not strange concerning the fiery trial which is to try you, as though some strange thing happened unto you: [13]But rejoice, inasmuch as ye are partakers of Christ's sufferings; that, when his glory shall be revealed, ye may be glad also with exceeding joy."

As for the fiery furnace, it seems the worst of all. Ruthless and savage, it leaps at every combustible thing that enters it and never relaxes its fury till it reduces it all to ashes. All that refuses to burn is melted down to a mass of helpless matter without will or purpose of its own. When everything is melted that will melt, and all is burned that will burn, then, and not until then, the furnace calms down and rests from its destructive fury.

God uses the hammer, the file, and the furnace in His holy work of preparing a vessel and to produce in him true humility. It is doubtful that God can bless anyone greatly until He has hurt him deeply.

Intercession:

The spirit of Jezebel hates intersession because interceding prayer has the power to break her stronghold. The beauty of the power of intercession is, people who could have been prey to the spirit of Jezebel are usually the ones that become mighty prayer warriors. They overcome that spirit through the power of inter-session and become mighty vessels in the hands of God. Our greatest weakness can become our greatest strength through the power of intercession.

I've seen women whose husbands beat them or left them who had every reason to distrust men and distrust authority but, instead, chose to submit themselves to their authority and became prayer warriors.

Submission to Authority:

Jezebel despises authority. I personally know what it means to run in fear. I know what it means to not let anyone get close to me. For many years I traveled around the world speaking and ministering all the while with walls up not truly submitting to authority on the deepest level. The ministry the Lord had given me had a glass ceiling limiting my effectiveness due to this partial submission.

What is partial submission? Submission as long as I agree with you and your advice agrees with my opinion. It's living your spiritual life feeling you have the right to a "second spiritual opinion;" which is seeking secondary counsel after your spiritual authority has counseled you and given you advise that goes against the grain of your wishes.

There is great joy in saying, "You're my pastor. I trust you; whatever you say, so be it." True spiritual authority and faith is found in submitting to authority.

Luke 7:6-9, "[6,7,8]Jesus went with them; but just before arriving at the house, the captain sent some friends to say, "Sir, don't inconvenience yourself by coming to my home, for I am not worthy of any such honor or even to come and meet you. Just speak a word from where you are, and my servant boy will be healed! I know, because I am under the authority of my superior officers, and I have authority over my men. I only need to say 'Go!' and they go; or 'Come!' and they come; and to my slave, 'Do this or that,' and he does it. So just say, 'Be healed!' and my servant will be well again!

"9Jesus was amazed. Turning to the crowd he said, "Never among all the Jews in Israel have I met a man with faith like this."[iv]

It is amazing that Jesus linked faith directly to submission. When we choose submission, there is a peace that comes. You don't have to fight or struggle anymore. You can just rest and enjoy the blessings of God that flow in this dimension of submission. This blessing spills over to your wife and children, even as they are in submission to you as the head of the household. This blessing spills over into your finances. It spills into your health. There's a beauty that comes when you choose submission.

There will be times that you feel a direction in which you feel God is calling you, or you've got a dream, and the authority God has placed in your life says, "It's not time," or "That's really not the direction that God wants to take you." You have two choices. Jump out ahead of the will of God and make it happen and fail, or choose submission and be successful in the Kingdom of God. You see, submission is a "dirty word" in today's society anymore. Oprah mocks it on television. Dr. Phil terms it "thinking for yourself." Our institutions of learning teach our children to challenge authority, to challenge absolutes, to challenge everything.

The Apostolic Church should not be dictated to by these mind-sets but, rather, by what "thus saith the Word of God."

Rebellion is a main key that opens the door to Jezebel influencing one's life. Rebellion is one of the roots.

1 Samuel 15:23, "For rebellion *is as* the sin of witchcraft, and stubbornness *is as* iniquity and idolatry. Because thou hast rejected the word of the LORD, he hath also rejected thee from *being* king."

Saul lost his kingdom due to partial obedience. That's the problem with some people. They think when they partially obey that they're right with God. God told Saul to kill all the Amalekites, and that was God's commandment to Saul. Saul made the mistake of taking God's commandment and obeying his own interpretation of it. This is the number one problem with people who deal with the spirit of Jezebel. They will partially obey what their authority told them to do (but only the part they agree with). They take everything that authority says and filters it through their interpretation of what they think should be done, not according to how they have been instructed, but by their interpretation of how it should be accomplished.

Saul said, "Let's keep King Agag and the best of the sheep, and of the oxen, and of the fatlings, and the lambs, and all the good things." Why? "I'm going to sacrifice to God." Every act of self-will and disobedience, or partial obedience, always has behind it a spiritual justification.

The true root of the matter is all about submission. It's all about obeying the Word of God. Partial obedience can get you into worse trouble than outright complete disobedience. Why? When you're disobeying and you're in sin, you know you're wrong. When you're only partially obeying, you convince yourself you're justified because at least you're doing something. Many in partial obedience say, "At least I'm going to church. At least I'm sitting on the pew." Those things are wonderful but, my friend, the only thing that gives you the favor and promises of God is complete obedience to His Word.

Saul kept back the cattle because he was just trying to strengthen his kingdom. To make things worse, when the prophet Samuel confronted him, Saul cast the blame upon the people. In response to Saul's partial obedience, God said, "Okay, Saul, because you only partially obeyed Me, now you and your sons will have no part of the kingship," and no part of Saul's lineage ever reigned as king from that day forward.

We create dysfunction and chaos for our children and our children's children when we choose to live our lives in partial obedience. We need to choose complete obedience. Reject the spirit of rebellion and embrace the spirit of obedience. The word 'rebellion' means insurrection and defiance.

When dealing with disobedient people influenced by the spirit of Jezebel, the issue you are presently dealing with is not ever the real issue. The true issue in all of these instances is control. Rebellion means revolt, mutiny, and insubordination. What is insubordination? It is lack of respect for authority and always finding a way to go around your leader's wishes and commands.

Saul prayed to God, but God didn't answer him that day (see 1 Samuel 14:37). So what did Saul do? He didn't wait to talk to God. He went and did his own work because he had the spirit of Cain, the spirit of self-will. This began the downward trend; Saul never again checked with his authority – God – for another battle or another decision. As king, he performed every decision based on what he thought was best. What a way to run a kingdom! Insubordination is to know a direct commandment, something you know should be done a certain way but choosing instead to do it the way you want. That's rebellion plain and simple. I've known people that at every turn of the hat argued with their authority. There is a blessing, even if you don't agree with your authority, to "look yes" in the public eye. It takes a truly spiritual man or woman to follow their leader's direction from their heart even when they may not agree. This kind of submission brings peace to a home and peace to a church.

Matthew 25:23 tells us, *". . . Well done, good and faithful servant; thou hast been faithful . . . ."* When we've proven ourselves faithful in small areas, then God can trust us with greater things. There are some people who want position, they want power, but they can't even obey in the small things. In every little thing they're constantly arguing, defying, justifying, doing their own way, and walking in the way of Cain and Korah. Now let me tell you about Cain and Korah.

Jude 11, *"Woe unto them! for they have gone in the way of Cain, and ran greedily after the error of Balaam for reward, and perished in the gainsaying of Core."*

Cain brought his sacrifice the way he wanted to. These are people who pay tithes the way they want to pay them, not according to the first fruits commandment of the Word. "Well, I'll pay tithes on what's left after I pay my bills." Or, "I'll catch up on my tithing when I have the finances."

I'm sure the offering from Cain was a nice offering, but it wasn't the way God said to bring it. God rejected Cain's offering but honored Abel's. Why? Simple obedience. There's beauty in taking teaching and saying, "God, if your Word says it this way, then that's the way I'm going to do it. If your Word goes against the way I want to do things, I will submit myself. I'm not going to choose the way of Cain. I'm not going to go my own way, but I'm going to choose the way of blessings!" Abel was blessed; Cain wasn't blessed.

Genesis 4:1-3, "¹And Adam knew Eve his wife; and she conceived, and bare Cain, and said, I have gotten a man from the LORD. ²And she again bare his brother Abel. And Abel was a keeper of sheep, but Cain was a tiller of the ground. ³And in process of time it came to pass, that Cain brought of the fruit of the ground an offering unto the LORD."

The problem with people that are plagued with the spirit of Cain is they're constantly doing good works or good things but not under the proper authority or process. They walk around with wounded spirits and say, "I always try to do those things that are good for God's kingdom, but I'm always getting corrected."

The problem is they're bringing an offering but not the way God told them to. Their response to correction is not repentance but to say, "Well, at least I'm trying to do something, but you don't appreciate that." That's how Cain felt. He came and brought an offering to God, but God had said from the beginning, if you offer an offering, then you must offer a lamb or something of blood. That's what God said. Cain said, "I'll bring the best food I've got." Unfortunately, although it was his best, it was not according to the commandment of God.

On the other hand, Abel brought his best according to the commandment of God and received respect. Genesis 4:4,5, "⁴And Abel, he also brought of the firstlings of his flock and of the fat thereof. And the LORD had respect unto Abel and to his offering:" He had respect. "⁵But unto Cain and to his offering he had not respect."

Instead of falling down and asking God why what he did was wrong and seeking to make it right, the spirit of Cain got very angry. The Bible says he was very wroth.

The spirit of Cain will go to everybody and tell them how they are being mistreated when Pastor has to deal with them because they did something that was good, but they did it wrong, they broke rules, and didn't submit themselves to the chain of command and authority. Instead of simply submitting and doing things the right way, they refuse to repent and will just stir up trouble.

The only way to get healing is to have Jezebel exposed. When you get the cancer out, then you can be healed. Cain got upset and went and killed his brother. All Cain would have had to do at this point was say, "Oh God, you don't want bananas and pomegranates and figs. You want a blood sacrifice." All he had to do was make a trade with Abel to make the sacrifice right. Conditional obedience never makes it in God's kingdom. "Well, I would pay my tithes, I would go to church, or I would be faithful, but I have a special situation that doesn't allow me to obey." Cain could have taken his fruit and traded them with Abel for a lamb.

It was not in Cain's heart to do it God's way. Instead, he grew angry and bitter at his brother's blessings, so he sought to destroy his brother.

You can't just live your life any way you want to. That's why there are rules and regulations. That's why there are commandments in God's Word. You can't just do whatever you want; you must live according to the Word of God if you want God's favor on your life. To live lawless is to live a life in rebellion against God. I don't care how much you say "I'm blessed," you won't be blessed. You break God's laws, and God doesn't bless you. See, we want a blessing "just because." You need to have God's respect for God to look down and say, "I honor that person." You've got to live right. Now, He still loves you. He'll always love you. But you can be anointed and not be blessed. You can live anointed and not be blessed.

Jude 12a, "These are spots in your feasts of charity, when they feast with you, feeding themselves without fear: clouds *they are* without water, ..."

They want everyone to serve them but they won't serve anybody. They take advantage of people's love and good will. They take and they take and they never give. They are clouds without water. They look like a cloud, they sound like a cloud, but after about 10 months of sitting on a pew you scratch your head because they never produce water. They look like a great Christian but then when you start watching their life there's no fruit ever. No blessings of God ever. They're constantly in financial ruin. They never can get ahead. They walk around talking about how bitter they are. "Everyone else is blessed but me." They're clouds without water because of the spirit of Cain.

Instead of repenting and changing their ways and seeing God's blessings come, they keep justifying, making excuses, and blaming everybody else for their problems. ". . . clouds *they are* without water, carried about of winds; trees whose fruit withereth, without fruit, twice dead, plucked up by the roots;" (Jude 12b).

These all are the symptoms of the spirit of Cain, which is under the stronghold of Jezebel, "raging waves of the sea." When you're in a boat on the sea and the winds are raging all around, all you can do is hang on. Some people's lives are so tumultuous; they're always in a storm, always upside down, all because of a spirit of Cain that refuses to submit. Self-will – "I'll do it my way," and they'll skirt around the issue every time. They'll blame everyone else, even make the leadership

Defeating the Spirit of Jezebel

look bad for calling their hand on their rebellion and their self-will. "Wandering stars . . ."

When someone has the spirit of Jezebel and doesn't know that you love them, when you reach out to try and work with them, they run. As long as they can keep the wool pulled over your eyes and make you think the person they're presenting to you is who they are, the second you find out who they really are and start dealing with them, if they don't know assuredly that Pastor loves them and cares about their future, they become wandering stars.

Church to church, city to city, state to state. They carry their story from place to place, and they can tell you a list going back 10 pastors of everything that has been done wrong to them.

They're wandering stars. I've had wandering stars float through the church I pastor. And I've sat in my office for three hours as they unveiled their story of injustice and being done wrong. I've always said the same thing to everyone who's walked through the doors of this church. "I'm so sorry that pastor did that to you. I'm so sorry that took place, but don't carry that into this church. Hang that stuff up, let it go and let me work with you." Then I look them in the eye and say, "Now we're in for a rough ride because you've not learned how to submit to authority. You've put up your guard saying, 'I don't have to submit because I was done wrong.' Somewhere, be it one month from now or one year from now, you're going to have to submit."

God puts us through tests sometimes to see if we'll obey. You cannot be anointed with authority without obeying. You cannot have great authority and great faith and God trust you and use you until you learn to obey. If you don't submit, then you will be a wandering star. You'll go around saying, "No one has ever given me a chance." You'll go from church to church with your story.

Wandering stars. Wandering stars are never used of God. They need to submit and ask God to help them not to go in the way of Cain but to break the spirit of Jezebel off their mind and spirit so they can be used of God.

Saul was anointed, Saul was king, but you find nowhere in Saul's kingdom where blessings came. He just kept running further and further from God. Why? Because he had the spirit of Cain on him. He wouldn't obey. God told him to kill all the Amalekites. He took that and did it his way. That got him in trouble. Anytime you choose the way of Cain you get in trouble even if you're doing a good work. Cain was doing a great work. He was offering a sacrifice to God, but he was doing it his way.

Now, about the gainsaying of Korah. The word 'gainsaying' in the original literally means the rebellion of Korah. The NIV version records Jude 11 this way:

"Woe to them! They have taken the way of Cain; they have rushed for profit into Balaam's error; they have been destroyed in Korah's rebellion"[v]

Korah missed a very valid point, and that is, God does not choose leadership based on ability. He chooses leadership based first on character and secondly His purpose. Korah was probably a better speaker than Moses. Korah was probably very influential and charismatic. He could probably just "wow" people. He was everybody's friend, personality plus. He knew everybody. Old Moses was a recluse. Korah, when he walked in the room, was probably the life of the party. Everybody liked Korah.

Moses, I don't know about him; he disappears for forty days at one time. He's supposed to be leading us to Canaan land and where's he at? Off somewhere in some mountain. Korah probably spoke eloquently while Moses stuttered. Slow of speech, the Bible says. Korah had the power to raise up insurrection. Korah went to all the influential people of the congregation and caused them to rise up, and they gathered themselves together against Moses and against Aaron and said, "You take too much upon you. Moses, you've got too much authority. You think you're God's man. We're all anointed; as a matter of fact, we're just as anointed as you are." That's the spirit of Korah, the spirit of rebellion.

The principle is not whether you hear from God or not. The truth is, if you weren't chosen by God, then honor the man God has chosen. God chose Moses. That's where the issue is. It's not whether you're anointed or not anointed, whether you hear from God or don't hear from God, or whether you have ability or don't have ability. It's whom did God choose and whom did God put in authority. Korah had a great case with the people, but his case was very poor to God because God did not choose Korah. Everything he's saying is true: Yes, God's people are anointed; yes, God's people are holy; yes, God's anointing is upon them; but God has always and will always work through His appointed authority. He will never work around it. God always works through His appointed authority.

Notice Moses' humble response to the rebellion of Korah:

Numbers 16:4, "And when Moses heard *it*, he fell upon his face:"

Moses didn't jump up and say, "Hey! I'm the leader here!" If you've got to keep telling people who's in authority, then you're not an authority. If you've got to keep reminding people who's in charge, then you've got a problem.

Moses fell on his face before God. He said, "God, it's in your hands. Tomorrow the Lord's going to show who is His." Moses had a serious problem on his hands. Korah had stirred up 250 renowned princes. These weren't just people, these were people who were respected and renowned. But notice in verse 21, the Lord spoke to Moses and said, "Moses and Aaron, separate yourselves from among the congregation that I may consume them in a moment." This is how God feels about spirits of insubordination and insurrection.

These are people who have no problem talking against authority behind the scenes just because they don't agree with them and stirring others toward their rebellious cause. If Moses had stepped back, they'd have been gone. Look at the next verse: "And they fell upon their faces, and said, O God, the God of the spirits of all flesh, shall one man sin, and wilt thou be wroth with all the congregation?"

This is one reason why I'm so tight with leadership. One person in leadership can do more damage than a hundred sitting on the pew when their spirit is not in subjection and submission. Moses said, "God, you're going to destroy the whole congregation because of one man's sin?" Notice in verse 28, this is so awesome. This shows the humility of Moses' leadership. Moses didn't stand up and demand his rights. He didn't demand that people respect him. Notice the power of humility. Humility was how Moses defeated the spirit of Jezebel. That's what kind of spirit that was driving Korah. He didn't defeat it with power. He didn't overcome it with an army. No. Humility has more power than rebellion and arrogance could ever have.

Numbers 16:28-35, "²⁸And Moses said, Hereby ye shall know that the LORD hath sent me to do all these works; for *I have* not *done them* of mine own mind. ²⁹If these men die the common death of all men, or if they be visited after the visitation of all men; *then* the LORD hath not sent me. ³⁰But if the LORD make a new thing, and the earth open her mouth, and swallow them up, with all that *appertain* unto them, and they go down quick into the pit; then ye shall understand that these men have provoked the LORD.

³¹And it came to pass, as he had made an end of speaking all these words, that the ground clave asunder that was under them: ³²And the earth opened her mouth, and swallowed them up, and their houses, and all the men that *appertained* unto Korah, and all *their* goods. ³³They, and all that *appertained* to them, went down alive into the pit, and the earth closed upon them: . . ."

God does not treat lightly the spirit of rebellion. He abhors it. It is as the spirit of witchcraft.

"³⁴And all Israel that *were* round about them fled at the cry of them: for they said, Lest the earth swallow us up *also*. ³⁵And there came out a fire from the LORD, and consumed the two hundred and fifty men that offered incense."

When you choose to step back and say, "God, this is yours. I'm not going to fight or fuss or struggle or sit there and argue until I'm red in the face with someone who doesn't see it my way. Lord, it's your church." That's a very fearful thing when it happens. God will not spare until the whole spirit is purged.

If we don't choose to deal with these spirits as a congregation, God will deal with them as the Chief Shepherd.

What are the blessings of submission? What are the blessings of obedience? In Matthew 25:23, the blessings are when you've been faithful over a few things. Let me tell you the type of leadership that I came up under. If my pastor came to me and said, "Brother Arcovio, I need you to go out there and sweep that parking lot and pick up all the trash by the fence." If I walked out there, swept the broom twice, and picked up a piece of trash, then this would show I was not willing to obey, and that I could not ever be trusted in the pulpit. I could not be trusted. You've got to prove yourself faithful in the small things. Proof of my willingness to obey from the heart would be for me to sweep the parking lot till you could eat off its surface and pick up every speck of trash in sight.

As a leader, if you desire to be a man of God, but you're always late to church, or you're always skipping important leadership meetings, if you're always hit and miss with your tithes and offerings, and you're lax about your passion for prayer and souls, you will not be used of God or be able to lead people to greater things. People don't follow leaders with no character.

Kick Cain and Korah out the front door and say, "Cain, you're not welcome here. I'm not doing it my way. Korah, you have no part in my home. I'm not going to live by rebellion." Through obedience we're blessed. If you can't even run with the footmen, you'll never make it with the horsemen. You won't even get in the saddle. Through obedience we're blessed with authority.

When you are in submission and you are obedient, God blesses you with authority, but when you are disobedient, you become stripped of authority. Rebellion is witchcraft. You don't have to wear a big pointy hat and ride on a broom to be involved with witchcraft. Witchcraft can make its way into the church and appear spiritual. A spirit is behind rebellion, and it's not the Holy Spirit. Rebellion says, "I will not do it!" when given biblical instruction.

In this world, sometimes we need to slow things down. We have to look at a word and walk around it a couple of times to really catch the full meaning of it. You see, the opposite of obedience is not disobedience. Disobedience is a lack of obedience. The opposite of obedience is rebellion.

In Mark 3 when the multitude came about Jesus, they said, "Behold your mother and brethren." And He said, "Who is my mother and brethren? Whosoever does the will of God, the same is my mother." It's all about doing the will of God. When you insist on your own way, you're just not in the family. To be a part of the family, you've got to do His will. Read it.

Some of the things that work through the spirit of Jezebel are: intimidation, manipulation, domination, and legalism. Legalism is feeling like, because you have some type of a standard, that you are better than someone else. You look down your nose at people. You judge people. Guilt and condemnation are both fruit of the spirit of Jezebel.

Galatians 3:1, "O foolish Galatians, who hath bewitched you, that ye should not obey the truth, before whose eyes Jesus Christ hath been evidently set forth, crucified among you?" 'Bewitched' means to be fascinated by a false representation.

Zechariah's vision:

Zechariah 1:18-21, "[18]Then lifted I up mine eyes, and saw, and behold four horns. [19]And I said unto the angel that talked with me, What *be* these? And he answered me, These *are* the horns which have scattered

Judah, Israel, and Jerusalem. [20]And the LORD shewed me four carpenters. [21]Then said I, What come these to do? And he spake, saying, These *are* the horns which have scattered Judah, so that no man did lift up his head: but these are come to fray them, to cast out the horns of the Gentiles, which lifted up *their* horn over the land of Judah to scatter it."

While these verses do have application in eschatology, there is a spiritual application. These 4 horns represent 4 powers that had scattered Israel. The horn is a symbol of power, strength, and might. There are powers and authorities in every region and city whose purpose is to scatter people and prevent the unity of the church. Many pastors today are frustrated due to the enemy's scattering and dividing efforts. No sooner is a church formed and gathered than the scattering spirit strikes. Pastors who have pastored for 25 years and never saw more than a few members leave are dismayed at the uprising of rebellion, disloyalty, and scattering that these horns of strife, division, and rebellion have accomplished in this present hour, and all are the general workings of Jezebel. Until these horns are dealt with, the people of God will remain scattered and not be able to lift their heads. This represents oppression and bondage. The apostolic, growing anointing will destroy these horns in Jesus Name!

When God comes to give us tune-ups, it's not that we're bad. He recognizes all the wonderful good things that are going on. Still He says, but now let's work with that engine that's missing a few beats here and there. That smoke coming out of the carburetor, let's work on that. He loves us so much He won't leave us in our faults and flaws. He'll constantly draw us toward perfection and drawing closer to him, and that's the difference between just striving for excellence and having obedience. You can be excellent and not be obedient. The business world strives for excellence but often doesn't truly care about the people they are serving. Most businesses in this day only care about the bottom line – the amount of profit they can make.

Obedience is where you face the Word of God square and say, "Okay, God, I want to obey You according to the Word of God."

This principle is what God was trying to get through to the Church of Thyatira. He told them they had all these great things, patience and works, greater now even than they were before. But He said, *"I have a few things against thee, because thou sufferest that woman Jezebel, which calleth herself a prophetess, to teach and to seduce . . ."*

The person that has the spirit of Jezebel on them completely thinks they're spiritual. This is why it's so difficult to deal with people that have the spirit of Jezebel. It's because there is a measure of anointing in their life. There is a measure of spirituality. You can't deny it. God does not remove it because another spirit is working behind the scenes. That spirit must be eradicated, and the person must go forth in their anointing and continue doing the work of God. The spirit has got to be exposed. When you face the spirit of Jezebel, the spirit of Jezebel will try to talk it's way out. It'll testify to everything it's doing; it'll give you Scriptures and tell you, "I had a dream last night; I had a vision, God spoke to me." You'll sit there and think, "Wow, what they're saying makes sense." They'll give you just enough Scripture to try to convince you of their spirituality. (The devil loves to quote Scripture, but he'll misquote it or he'll misapply it.)

The first thing the spirit of Jezebel tries to do is discredit the authority. They'll strengthen their position by gathering around them as many people as they can to see it their way to try to "build a case" against the pastor or leader. They'll even try to turn it into a personality conflict. "Oh well, we just don't get along."

The Lord said, "Nevertheless I have a few things against you because you allow this spirit to remain" (see Revelation 2:20). Conventional wisdom in this hour says sometimes it's easier not to rock the boat, not to step out and deal with something because you don't want trouble. That's one of the things the spirit of Jezebel uses. It uses harassment, humiliation, and manipulation. If it's a wife that tries to control a husband, then that spirit will come up in her, and she will give him enough heartache and cause enough trouble that if he tries to stand up as the spiritual leader of that home and tries to do something he'll wish he'd never done it.

I've pastored husbands where the entire home was out of order and where the spirit of Jezebel had completely bound the wife to where she dictated and forced every decision in the home. When they come to church, she stands there and sweetly says, "Oh, I'm in submission to my husband." But the husband and children all know it's not true. They know who rules the roost, and you better do it this way or you are going to be sorry. I've seen men sit back and let that spirit operate, and I've told them, "You are the priest of your home, you're the spiritual leader. You need to rise up and say, 'No, we're not going to bring that garbage in the house.'" And they'd say, "Oh, but Pastor, you don't know my wife. I'd rather have peace. I've gone this way before and it just turns the whole home upside down."

As the spiritual leader, you are responsible to start fasting and praying and asking God to break this thing from off your home. You can get more done through prayer and fasting. You get more done with honey than you do with vinegar. So, as the leader of the home, it's not that you walk in and turn the house up-

Defeating the Spirit of Jezebel

side down and stomp around and say, "I'm the authority in this house, and you're going to do what I say." That's Adam. You don't need Adam. Adam messes things up. To be the authority in the home, you need to stand strong and say this is how it should be, and I'm going to pray. Begin to fast and pray, and you can break more yokes off the home through prayer and fasting than by any other means.

Back to verse 20, "... *she calls herself a prophetess.*" Don't be surprised when you start dealing with the spirit of Jezebel in your home if it rises up and starts becoming spiritual on you.

There are many sexual sins that plague the household that has the spirit of Jezebel. There are certain sexual sins that will attack children under the influence of the spirit of Jezebel in the household. It will attack husbands; even attack wives that deal with a spirit of Jezebel. Young men that come up under a spirit of Jezebel become susceptible to spirits of homosexuality. Young woman become susceptible to lesbianism. When a mother dominates the household, forces every decision that's made, controls everybody and everything around her, and refuses to submit to the authority of her husband, she molds that son and confuses the sexuality. Young people that come out from under the spirit of Jezebel are confused sexually. They don't know what the rules are in the household. They've been so twisted for so many years. And most young men that come out from the spirit of Jezebel resent woman, hate them, and are harsh toward them. They grow up resenting all women, and for most men who get into pornography it is because pornography is the defilement of a woman. It's the degradation.

If any woman in her right mind were to be exposed to countless men, she would feel filthy and degraded. Young ladies that are subjected to the spirit of

Jezebel in the home grow up confused and become overly aggressive, too aggressive. Because the roles are so confused, they fall prey. They get caught up in these sins and don't even know why. I have counseled young men who've been bound to homosexuality or pornography that don't know how to love women properly or how to treat a woman with respect and honor.

I ask questions, and two things stand out the strongest. First of all it is a non-existent father. Either he was someone so consumed with life that he was never there, or someone who left home and separated, or he might be a father that was there but was so harsh and rejecting that the child could never bond with him constantly being slammed to the ground and pushed away. This, combined with a dominating, manipulating, controlling, and ruling mother, develops the spirit of homosexuality and the tendency toward it. Then the spirit comes and preys on them. I've seen people battle this, and they don't even understand why. All of this is the fruit of the spirit of Jezebel. Now do you understand why it's so important to confront the spirit?

The spirit of Jezebel can exercise its authority and not even be in the home. I've known grown woman that have been married for 10 years whose mothers felt they still controlled their marriage from afar. That's the spirit of Jezebel. The spirit of Jezebel is against the family, against the unity of the family, and it's all about "my authority," "who I am," and "what I say, goes." It can work destruction. I've seen mothers-in-law destroy marriages quicker than you can blink an eye because they would not leave their daughters alone. They felt that they still had a right and authority. I've even seen mothers that were so insecure and wanting so much to keep control of her daughter that she even encouraged the daughter to divorce her husband because that would accomplish her purpose of bringing that daughter back to her. That's a despicable, abominable spirit of Jezebel from hell, and it's got to be bound and cast out from the family.

By the way, if you've got children that are married, it's not your business to even get involved in their marriage. It does not matter how much good you think you can do. You're better off to stay out of the marriage, pray and fast for your children, and only offer advise when it is asked for. That's why it's usually not healthy to have family members living in the home full time. Now if it's for a time or for a season okay, but to live in your married children's home you're going to naturally get too involved. You're better off as parents to back off and let your children make their own mistakes. Now if they come to you, that's different. But resist the desire to offer advise that's not asked for. Mothers need to be careful. You can be talking to little Sally and she can start talking about the little spat or problem that every marriage has, and then you start getting resentment in your heart against that man, and you start feeding that woman bitterness against her husband. Before you know it, you are joining with her against her husband to destroy that marriage. You're better off just backing off and praying for them and not allowing them to sit down and pour out all their anger. If they do, you need to start praying with them and say, "You need to restore your relationship."

If that daughter gets mad and leaves her husband and walks to your house and says, "Bless God, let me tell you what he did tonight," you need to say, "Honey, I'm sure he did something bad, but you need to turn yourself around, go back home, and we'll talk about it tomorrow." Don't you put her on the couch in your living room; you're not helping that marriage. I will say, this all is excluded if someone is being physically violent. If the wife is being beaten or something physical, then by all means, she needs to get out.

Unrepented acts of the spirit of Jezebel will even cause an open door to sickness and affliction. I've seen people who were bound by the spirit of Jezebel refuse to repent, then other spirits would come under that spirit as the spirit of infirmity. It doesn't mean that everyone who gets sick is bound by the spirit of Jezebel, but when all the things line up, many times the result of it is the spirit of infirmity walks through the door, and people are sick all the time. And you look at them and wonder why they are always sick. You can trace it back to a lack of submission, to rebellion, and to the spirit of self-will.

Some of the spirits that work under the spirit of Jezebel are fear and humiliation as in a wife humiliating her husband. Wives, don't ever humiliate your husband in public. Don't ever say something demeaning about him. *Don't get together with other wives and talk about your husband's sexual inability. You are destroying his manhood.* Protect your husband. Honor him with your words. Even if he is a "worthless no-good," you're not going to change him by destroying his credibility and his honor to others because you think you've got a right to vent. You're driving him further from you; so don't be surprised when he doesn't come home with a bouquet of flowers that night. You can use your tongue to destroy every ounce of love he has in his heart for you. Learn to honor him even if you don't agree. Respect him. Teach your children to respect him.

We live in a society that demeans the husband. There are sitcoms out that represent husbands as bumbling fools. Comic strips that are supported by the women's lib depict men as ignorant, inept, unable to be a father, and just bumbling idiots. They've got some strong woman that comes in that is so intelligent that brings it all together. It's a design of Hollywood and hell itself to destroy the sanctity of the home. Even if your husband doesn't bring in good money, don't mock him for that, don't berate him. Don't make him feel as lesser of a man. Even if you're bringing in more money than he is, he's still the breadwinner of the home.

I was reading a report about a church that ran 2,500 people, and the pastor called a week's prayer vigil. Only 25 people showed up and by the end of that prayer week, out of a church of 2,500, there were only 17 left praying. The very next week they had a night where they rewarded people for service in the church and more than 1,500 people showed up. Some people won't serve unless their names are in lights. This is a result of the spirit of Jezebel.

3 John 9, "I wrote unto the church: but Diotrephes, who loveth to have the preeminence among them, receiveth us not."

When leadership deals with a church and with a church issue that's afflicting many, many people, those that have the spirit of Diotrephes, which is simply the fruit of or an underlying spirit of the spirit of Jezebel, rise up and say, "Well, you know what, you all can do that, but I don't have to do it. I don't have to bring myself under the subjection of any man."

In Revelation 2:28 it states, *"And I will give him the morning star."* The Morning Star represents the Glory of God. How many want God's glory in your life?

Another response of the spirit of Jezebel is to never honor a man of God as being God's chosen man. Also it never recognizes the man of God bringing the preached Word as being the oracle or the mouthpiece of God. Jezebel chooses to only look at the natural man. Since Jezebel has problems with authority, everything

Defeating the Spirit of Jezebel

preached is responded to with, "Well, I just don't agree with what he says."

I Peter 4:11 states the principle of receiving a man of God as the oracle:

"If any man speak, *let him speak* as the oracles of God; if any man minister, *let him do it* as of the ability which God giveth: that God in all things may be glorified through Jesus Christ, to whom be praise and dominion for ever and ever. Amen."

The word 'oracles' found in 1 Peter 4:11 comes from the Greek word NT:3051 *logion (log'-ee-on)*; neuter of NT:3052; an utterance (of God):[vi]

'Oracles' literally means that when the man of God gets up and breaks the bread of life, it is as if God Himself is speaking to you. If you cannot receive it as the Word of God, then you will constantly battle with principles taught and brought forth as just a difference of opinion.

Hebrews 13:17, "Obey them that have the rule over you, and submit yourselves: for they watch for your souls, as they that must give account, that they may do it with joy, and not with grief: for that is unprofitable for you."

Jezebel hates this Scripture. "Who, me obey? No, not on your life. Don't have to." When Jezebel gets convicted enough about resisting God's Word, then they'll either attack the credibility of the person teaching or will attack the messenger. They attack the leadership to try to discredit them and to bring questions into people's minds about their credibility. My friend, if what I am writing is hitting home in your life, you need to submit and repent. Remember, it is easier to leave Jezebel working in your life than to seek God for change. But to experience deliverance, choose the hard road and seek change. If you will seek Him, He will help you find change.

In dealing with Jezebel, you must get past the fruit and deal with the root. You deal with the root when you repent, choose humility, choose submission, choose intercession, and choose to obey the prophet of God. I challenge you, if you will take these teachings and apply them to yourself, when you get past this season and the next season comes around there won't be any negative fruit you will have to deal with. No negative fruit in your family, no negative fruit in your home, and no negative fruit in your marriage. Some people go in constant cycles and seasons and years go by, and they still have the same problems they dealt with five years ago that they're still dealing with. Deal with the roots and when the next season comes, instead of bitterness, instead of financial difficulty, instead of lack of positive fruit, you'll have blessings, love, joy, peace, longsuffering, patience, and the favor of God. Think of the blessing, think of the favor of God. That's what happens when you make the right choices and choose to set in motion the things that will defeat Jezebel in your life and in the lives of those you love.

May the truths in this book set you and your church free and, in doing so, set your city free and aflame with the revival fires of God! Amen!

Endnotes:

---

[i] Biblesoft's New Exhaustive Strong's Numbers and Concordance with Expanded Greek-Hebrew Dictionary. Copyright (c) 1994, Biblesoft and International Bible Translators, Inc.
[ii] Author unknown
[iii] Webster's Dictionary
[iv] The Living Bible
[v] New International Version
[vi] Biblesoft's New Exhaustive Strong's Numbers and Concordance with Expanded Greek-Hebrew Dictionary. Copyright (c) 1994, Biblesoft and International Bible Translators, Inc.

ACKNOWLEDGMENTS

Many books are written from a scholarly reference. *Defeating the Spirit of Jezebel* is mostly written as a result of 30 years of experience ministering around the globe and 10 years experience pastoring. This book is birthed from a vision to put in the hands of God's spiritual warriors a handbook on spiritual warfare.

I dedicate this book to the late Prophet T. W. Barnes, who was my mentor.

Thank you for the wonderful church body I pastor in Saint Joseph, Missouri, for releasing me time and again to minister around the world. Thank you to the spiritual Jehu's God is raising up in This last day.

Thank you for my sweet children Ariella and Jonathon for dedicating your lives to God and following in our footsteps.

Thank you to Lori Felzien for your rough draft editorial work. Thank you to Jonathan McCune for your final editorial work.

Most of all, thank you to my faithful friend and saviour Jesus; you make all things possible.